CREATING
SMALL GARDENS

*

CREATING
SMALL GARDENS

*

ROY STRONG

Conran Octopus

This book sets out to achieve one modest objective – to release those who have a small garden from treating it in terms of a series of clichés. It is unashamedly design-orientated, responding outdoors to the impulse that has transformed the indoors of so many homes during the last few years. I make no apology for what is a purely personal anthology of alternative treatments – dreams – for small sites. Being a design gardener rather than a plantsman myself this book would not have been compiled without the assistance of Susan Conder and Jasmine Taylor, for which I am more than grateful.

Roy Strong

First published in 1986 by
Conran Octopus Limited
37 Shelton Street
London WC2H 9HN

Text copyright © Roy Strong 1986
Illustrations copyright © Conran Octopus Limited 1986
This paperback edition
published 1989 by
Conran Octopus Limited

Art Director: Douglas Wilson
Managing Editor: Jasmine Taylor
Art Editor: Jill Raphaeline
Contributing Editor: Susan Conder
Picture Researcher: Shona Wood
Illustrators: Liz Pepperell (The Garden Studio),
John Davies
Editorial Assistant: Laura Down

The editors would also like to thank the following:
Russell Gordon-Smith, Mary Trewby and Brian Carter.

ISBN 1 85029 185 3

Typeset by Tradespools Limited

Printed and bound in Spain

CONTENTS

*

INTRODUCTION

*

I came to gardening late. When I was thirty-five we bought a small house in the country. 'Don't talk to me about that garden,' I remember saying to my wife, as I took in half an acre of lawn and rose beds and an adjoining field in which, mercifully, cows were contentedly munching the grass (it was let to a farmer). It was, in fact, my second garden. My first had been a tiny one at the back of a Regency Gothic house in Brighton, which I had paved and filled with terracotta pots and urns planted with herbs and shop-bought geraniums. The activity was more like perpetual first aid than inspired horticulture. In retrospect, that garden was merely putting a toe into an ocean into which I was shortly to plunge.

*

But back to the country and my first 'real' garden. Fifteen years on, there is virtually nothing left of the garden as we found it. At the start we really had very little idea and our initial forays consisted of planting welcome donations of shrubs and plants from friends – mostly in the wrong places – and hoping for the best. The advice from the local nursery man to plant poplars was nearly disastrous: their suckers are still undermining the drive. The fatal telephone call from the farmer saying that he was removing his cows from the field fuelled further folly. But the idea of an overall plan or concept only came with the *tabula rasa* of that field combined with a foray into the garden history of renaissance England. Suddenly I became aware of the importance of design. My wife, Julia, on observing a level area of the vacant field, proffered the view that 'There must have been an old lawn tennis court there once'. She was right. We mowed back the long grass to reveal the plateau and that winter I planted a yew hedge around two thirds of it and then dug flowerbeds for roses.

Everyone who saw those eighteen-inch high sprigs of yew thought that we were mad and would certainly never live to see the hedge. Twelve years later I can sit in that garden, totally enclosed by an eight-foot high hedge, which I lovingly cut into piers and buttresses each August.

That rose garden marked the turning point. We realized that any garden must start with a design, a plan, a sense of structure and optical illusion before plants are selected.

*

I am not at all sure what prompted this gardening passion. Perhaps it was my wife who comes from a gardening family. Their third of an acre in a London suburb was a joy to see, with its flower-packed beds, its tiny greenhouse and neat vegetable patch. But I cannot say that the garden was a monument to design. More potent were the visits to country house gardens. I was then left with the problem of how to distil their labour-intensive grandeur to an area of more modest proportions. As a result, my approach has been, and continues to be, that of a designer and a romantic rather than a plantsman. My view of gardening is that of a set designer who sees his garden as one big stage. On it, the seasons are conceived as a series of tableau through which the visitor moves. It always seems important to me for anyone who has a garden to decide exactly what he or she wants from it. I have always wanted a sense of spectacle, illusion and style: as I learn more about plants I find them more and more interesting but, for me, they will always remain secondary to the design concept.

Once set on this path, it surprised me how little that was published on the subject was relevant. There were, of course, the grand designers and the not so grand ones attached to garden centres and nurseries, but there was no guiding hand for those who wanted to do it themselves. And the not so grand professional designers seemed in the death grip of island beds and municipal planting. There were a thousand books on how to lay crazy paving or cope with garden pests or grow prize chrysanthemums but none on attainable style in a modest patch.

This is pertinent because one of the most noticeable features of the last twenty years, and especially of the last decade, has been the boom in interior design. It is reflected in the endless decorating magazines and in the co-ordinated wallpapers, fabrics and paints now available. As a result, standards in interior design have improved across a wide range of the social spectrum. That raising of standards has yet to happen in the garden. For some reason, people cease to think about design as soon as they walk into the garden. Perhaps this is because nearly all garden books are horticulturally slanted, and so are garden centres and nurseries. If a nursery does have a garden attached to it, invariably it is planted as one large one. How much more useful it would be if nurseries and garden centres constructed a series of small gardens in the same way as shops display room settings: ones which are concerned with colour co-ordination; also ones which would solve the numerous problems that arise from planting a small area.

The twenty-four gardens I have included in this book have been chosen, therefore, for their very individual sense of style. Each one of them is different, not only as an expression of the taste of a particular owner but as a response to such circumstances as architecture, site and use. I do not see the gardens as offering package solutions but as providing a quarry of ideas and, in addition, practical information. Lift sections of someone else's garden but never the whole design, for your own garden must be yours. In any case, its idiosyncrasies should ensure that it is. Fortunately, no two plants ever grow in exactly the same manner.

*

The relationship of small garden design to interior decoration is an extremely valid one. No room can contain more than one co-ordinated theme. The smaller a garden is, the closer to a room it becomes, and the lesson on a unifying theme, reiterated throughout this book, is reinforced.

Not only should the design of the garden be pertinent to the architecture of the house but also to its interior design. Looking out from a window the garden becomes a 'wall' of an interior room. Mirrors reflect the exterior, also bringing the garden image indoors. A traditional cottage interior of oak, plasterwork and beams demands a traditional garden in drifts of old-fashioned flowers. A house full of Victoriana with swagged and frilled curtains and flower-decked wallpaper calls for a garden, perhaps of old roses, which continues the lush profusion in the open. A twentieth-century house with rooms filled with furniture in glass, leather and steel and walls hung with modern art suggests a garden of bold abstract shapes and forms in stone with asymmetrical planting.

This relationship between interior and exterior in design terms is a reassertion of an ancient norm. The great architects of the renaissance, the period in which western gardening was born, designed both the exteriors and interiors of their buildings, as well as the gardens. They were thought of as one. One of my aims is to make people think again in those terms when 'furnishing' even the smallest area of earth.

Garden design actually precedes the horticultural side of gardening. The idea of flowers as forming a major part of any garden is a relatively new one. It is certainly not part of the Japanese tradition which relies for its effects on stones, gravel, water and the most sparse of plantings. Nor did the great gardens of Europe in the sixteenth and seventeenth centuries depend for their impact on flowers. Instead, they relied on sculpting the terrain with paths, terraces and steps enlivened by clipped evergreens, hedges, trees, sheets of water, fountains and sculpture. These seemingly extravagant creations have much to teach us today about using simple ingredients. They remind us, too, of the satisfaction to be gained by a controlled arrangement of nature, one that requires little more than annual clipping and pruning.

Incidentally, I believe that it is important to be relaxed about gardening. If you fail to prune a shrub at exactly the right time it will probably not be disastrous. Likewise, if for some reason you may not be able to rush out and do the weeding regularly but only cope with periodic rescue work, do not worry. Once a garden becomes a burden it ceases to be a pleasure. And although gardening is work, it is also perpetual delight in terms of colour, fragrance and texture.

*

The creative development of the small garden is probably this century's greatest contribution to the art of gardening. Up until the middle of the last century, gardening was done on a huge scale – the great formal parterres of the baroque palace garden or the acres of an eighteenth-century English landscape park – and design ideas and principles reflected this.

Nowadays, gardening on such a vast scale is in the main confined to public spaces or to maintaining existing historical ensembles. We live in an age of the small garden, reflective of a more democratic society in which living is more modest and equal and in which gardeners are a declining breed. The vast majority of gardens are small ones. Yet how little literature they have evoked on the culture of their design, even though a small garden presents a design problem comparable to that within the walls of the house. The successful solution of both is an expression not only of personality but of taste, the creation of a harmonious environment which will give perpetual delight to the senses and, even in the case of a garden, a feeling of solid comfort and good living that extends outwards to everyone who sees it.

Good design is good housekeeping. It is the combination of an aesthetic effect with pragmatic practicality in terms of labour and maintenance. If you achieve that well may you rest, like the man in the Old Testament, beneath the shade of your vine and enjoy to the full the fruits of your labours.

The
ELEMENTS OF
DESIGN

*

Planning a garden is similar to decorating and furnishing
a house – it cannot be done without knowing what the
materials and techniques are at your desposal. These are
set out in the pages that follow, together with the initial
steps you need to take when you begin to orchestrate the
materials and techniques into a garden scheme. Live with
a garden for a year while you make your plan, then put it
into action over the winter months. The ensuing spring
will bring you the first fruits of your thought, planning
and labour.

ASSESSING REQUIREMENTS

*

It can take several years to create a really spectacular garden from scratch so consider time seriously as a factor before you plan anything. Is this the house in which you intend to live for the majority of your life, perhaps for as much as half a century, or is it a first home with a move envisaged in a few years? If it is a retirement home – and you happen to be pushing sixty-five – do not rush out and plant a formal garden of yew and box, unless you intend to leave it to someone else to enjoy.

The second time dimension is a more mundane one; the actual amount of it you intend to spend on your garden (on the assumption that there is no paid help). Is it to be a few hours at weekends or is it to be your consuming passion? This, again, should affect your choice of design. There is no point, for example, in embarking on an emulation of one of the more elaborate gardens in this book if you are not prepared to meet the physical input it demands.

There is a final point to be made about time and gardening; however much your garden is designed at the outset, always be prepared for alteration and modification at a later date. Time is one of the most wonderful but unpredictable allies in a garden and what may look right on a plan may look remarkably off-key as it grows, and vice versa. Be prepared as time passes to respond to its gestures in full.

THE GENIUS OF THE PLACE
A successful garden is immediately recognizable by its strong sense of identity. Everything there has purpose, either practical or aesthetic, combining to make a coherent picture. This is particularly true of small gardens which can rarely sustain more than one vision, whereas large ones can proliferate a variety of moods. The biggest decision to make is this one, and the will to follow it through for several years until it reaches maturity.

With your resources at your fingertips begin by looking at the architecture of your house and at neighbouring gardens. The latter will tell you much about local style and materials, and what grows in the soil. In a small

ABOVE A garden designed to be looked down on rather than lived in, a geometric pattern of clipped box with compartments filled with flowers. A high hedge ensures complete privacy.

LEFT A garden conceived with all the clutter and comfort of a living room in which to relax, with 'walls' of glossy evergreens and a soft abundance of bloom.

11

garden the house is never lost sight of and can never be planted out. You must start from it, even if one of your decisions is to smother it in roses, clematis and wisteria to conceal some of its uglier features. Whether it is built of wood, brick, stone or stucco, and whether it is in the farmhouse, cottage, classical, Gothic, Victorian, art deco, art nouveau, modern, or even post-modern style, all good garden design starts with the house and works out from it. The two must be treated as a single interconnecting unit.

INHERITING AN ESTABLISHED GARDEN

The same processes of analysis are relevant to an established garden. It is important in this case to carry out major amputations before your eye becomes accustomed to what initially appeared as visual aberration. But do not be too precipitate. Your predecessors are unlikely to have arrived at the existing garden purely by accident. What has previously grown and thrived should be noted and respected. Once again the materialization of your vision will require a careful marriage of resources, this time mature ones, to new input. In many ways there are enormous advantages in starting with an existing garden which may bring blessings such as mature trees. These should be cherished.

INTENDED USE

List in order of importance what you want from your garden: a tableau from the living room window; an outdoor room in which to eat and relax; a haven for birds and other wildlife; a shady retreat in which to sit; a compound in which to safely deposit the children; a secret hidden place; a source of garden produce for the freezer; a supplier of flowers for the house; or a purely romantic idyll. Add to these possibilities a list of drab necessities which are a part of modern living: the garage, parking space, compost heap, tool shed, fuel store, clothesline, workshop and bonfire site. These need to be conveniently placed for access and also hidden from view by walls and hedges. Work from both lists to marry your objectives with the remaining available space.

With a small garden it is unlikely that you will be able to make more than one total statement. Do not be surprised at this but work from it out into the details.

PLANNING

I cannot overemphasize the importance of a camera to anyone remotely interested in the art of gardening. Start by photographing the garden from as many viewpoints as possible. Include photos from the main windows of the house because, for most of the year, that is how you will see your garden. Draw a ground plan as near to scale as you can on graph paper. With these two resources you can decide at once on what you want to conceal – from the next-door neighbour to an offensive view – and, in addition, where to hide the services. This done, you are then in a position to consider what you want to do with the remaining available space.

It is always important to start with marking the main axes and vistas from the windows of the house upstairs and down. If you have a first-floor living room the pattern of the garden at ground level is crucial to its success. If your main living room is at street level the perspective of vistas at eye level will be the governing factor around which to arrange your design. Then think of the reverse view back to the house and consider how you might enhance its appearance with wall-trained shrubs, climbing plants and pergolas.

These main axes and vistas inevitably suggest where paths should fall or rather in the end lead. They also indicate what should be framed – controlling a view by focusing the eye through a garden arch, or trees and shrubs planted on each side, leading the eye on. By the time the main outlines of your garden fall into place, the next stage is to experiment on site using canes and pieces of string to mark on to the earth or grass the outline paths, beds and other features.

PLANNING PLANTS

Plants are cheaper than capital building works, but that is no excuse for impulse buying or random siting. As a general rule, the longer lived a plant is, and the larger its scale, the more care should go into its choice and positioning. And the smaller the garden, the more important forethought is.

Remember, in a garden centre, a tree that eventually reaches a height of four metres, or twelve feet, may look exactly the same as one that grows ten times that high.

If, because of finances, planting has to be done in stages, the first planting should include the major trees and hedges, if possible. The sooner they put roots down and begin to grow, the sooner your composition will materialize. These plants form the backbone of your garden, and within their framework, your can add infill shrubs, perennials, biennials, bulbs and, most fleeting of all, annuals. With perennials, biennials, bulbs and annuals, there is more room for experimentation. They cost less than trees and shrubs, and can be moved more easily, should a better position declare itself in the garden. Such plants are also shorter lived; with them, it is easy to correct, or at the very worst bury, your mistakes.

LEFT The garden as an
elegant outdoor formal *salon*.
Walls of yew hedging contain
furniture and symmetrically
placed terracotta urns with
box spheres and spirals.
Flowers are unnecessary.

LEFT The garden as a
plantsman's paradise. A
symphony of controlled colour
– creamy white into green –
including anaphalis,
verbascum, antirrhinums and
fennel.

13

SPRING

*

The utter simplicity and freshness of a wild planting of ordinary daffodils against an immaculate picket fence.

Spring can come in a rush, arrive in fits and starts or be a stately paced affair, according to country and climate. Spring can be early and it can as equally be late. Of all the seasons, spring remains the greatest miracle. Even in the tiniest patch of garden it never ceases to amaze when the first bright-green shoots appear. Although the days quickly lengthen and warmth returns, it is still often chilly. From that point of view, and an aesthetic one, it is important to plan spring to be seen from the windows.

Make sure that the plants lead the eye right through the garden. Tulips, for example, in the foreground, could be backed up by hyacinths in an urn in the middle distance and at the furthest boundary a small flowering tree such as *Malus* 'Golden Hornet' or, one of my favourites, *Amelanchier lamarcki*, with flowers like tiny white stars. In fact, flowering almond, plum, cherry or ornamental crab apple is a desideratum for any garden, but avoid the cliché of a forest of hectic pink cherry blossom produced by many of the Japanese hybrids. These rank as very boring trees for most of the year.

Bulbs present special problems for a small garden and their inclusion will depend on the nature of your design. Tall-growing tulips can be planted in formal blocks of colour, but if your garden is informal choose species tulips or, perhaps, early single- or double-flowered ones. Daffodils, narcissi, crocuses and scillas need informal planting in drifts and clumps. Thought must be given to the fact that in the case of naturalized bulbs the grass cannot be cut before the middle of summer.

Colour control in garden design is essential at all times of the year, but especially during spring. Violent colour means spring erupting rather than unfolding. The equation of the advent of spring with strong colour, especially yellows, oranges, reds and pinks, jammed together in a small space and screaming at each other, should be avoided. Keep to a graduated palette moving through various strengths of the same colour with only occasional splashes of the stronger tones.

Be cautious when choosing and juxtaposing azaleas, rhododendrons, camellias, forsythia or broom. There are so many shrubs that offer a softer, more dappled effect: the snowball bush (*Viburnum opulus*) or *V.* × *juddii* with the palest pink scented blooms, for example. There is no lack of choice, but in a small space you cannot afford to have any plant that does not provide interest in at least two out of the four seasons of the year. That is why lilac is such a mistake for a small garden: glorious in blossom time, deadly thereafter. In a confined area, flowering trees and shrubs should also provide attractive branch and leaf formation, or colour, berries and fruits in the autumn.

Spring in a more formal
garden style: tulips in box-
edged beds with irises beyond.
The architectural structure of
the garden's evergreens
ensure year-round interest
and provides a perfect foil for
seasonal plantings.

SUMMER

*

The problem for the small garden in summer is one of choice. At no other time of year is there such a glorious abundance of foliage and flowers from which to choose. Control of that cornucopia is all important and it will be radically affected by your style and objectives: formal or informal, low or high maintenance. In summer the garden becomes a room in which to wander, and not every effect has to be calculated as seen from the windows. For the next six months you will be perpetually moving through and sitting in your three dimensional picture savouring every effect close to. Smell – that neglected garden sense – will come much in use whether it is the heady sweetness of dianthus and night-scented stock or the more aromatic perfume of box and rosemary.

Controlled abundance is, I believe, the key. Unlike other seasons, summer is a time when the design concept can be quickly obscured, as plants grow out of shape or encroach paved areas. Then the designer's eye is called for, knowing instinctively where a line needs to be reinstated or where, in fact, it looks more delightful broken. Summer is the main time for hedge cutting, which I consider one of gardening's joys. Whether done with mechanical or hand shears, there are few greater pleasures than standing back and admiring your own work as you sculpt nature into shape. And it always occurs at the moment when the garden is just about to tip over into untidy disarray.

These are the months of the rose, about which I eulogize at length on pages 84–9. It is difficult to conceive of any garden without at least one, the perfect symbol of summer and responsive to every type of garden design. The rose can be formal, with carefully planted bushes orchestrated in a single colour. The rose can as equally be sweet confusion, tumbling, cascading and embowering pergolas, pavilions and walls.

In addition, these are also the months when perennials and annuals come to their apogee in the mixed borders which, however small, should never lack for interest or colour. The range of plants is enormous: lupin, delphinium, mullein, campanula, geranium, astilbe, gaillardia, helianthus, erigeron, peony, phlox, day lily. The range of shrubs is equally as large: philadelphus, choisya, daphne, escallonia, potentilla, weigela, hebe, cistus, hypericum, deutzia, senecio, lavender. And then there are the climbers: hybrid clematis, honeysuckle, jasmine and passionflower. For the first-time gardener it is all rather overwhelming and looks far more complicated than it is. Every one of us starts in the same way; all of us make mistakes and sustain casualties. Plunge in and hope for the best and start by overplanting. It is always cheering to have too much rather than too little and you can make adjustments later. And never waste time trying to get something to grow if it will not.

Summer is so demanding in terms of work and so prolific that it is easy to forget to take stock of one's composition, examining the balance of the total garden scene and jotting down the corrections that should be made during winter. And remember that a lot of first aid can be achieved by buying annuals from a nursery and just popping them in to fill the blank spaces. This is the only season when one can successfully 'cheat' in the garden, and buy in instant colour.

ABOVE An old-fashioned, stately line of pink, rose and crimson hollyhocks combine to present the fullness of summer in a cottage garden.

RIGHT The lush profusion of summer with its cascades of blooms. Notice the softness of colour with only a few flecks of stronger tones.

16

AUTUMN

*

Autumn I consider to be the most romantic of the seasons. The frantic growth of the previous months slows down, the light becomes soft and golden, and the garden enters its slow annual death in a way that combines serene beauty with an undeniable poignancy. There is a sense of home-coming as the fruits are gathered in. There is a wistful sadness in the red and gold leaves on the trees and shrubs; one day they glow like beacons in the autumn sun but overnight can fall to the ground, felled by an early frost. Fallen leaves are a pleasure to look at, and there is that most nostalgic of autumn activities, the bonfire.

In terms of planting autumn runs as a counterpoint to spring. Those who have fruit trees will now enjoy the sight of fruit ripening. In the Renaissance, fruit trees were often planted in the flower garden for they were rightly

ABOVE Autumnal colours of the ornamental vine (*Vitis coignetiae*).

RIGHT Japanese maples, sedums and polygonum create perfect harmony.

18

The smoke tree (*Cotinus coggygria*) produces an unrivalled, if ephemeral, display.

regarded not only as a source of food but as decorative in their own right. That tradition needs to be restored. Ornamental crab apples also fruit, bright yellow on 'Golden Hornet' and pale yellow flushed with red on 'John Downie'. Both make marvellous jelly. The ornamental rowans, too, are laden with berries: pure white for *Sorbus cashmiriana*, bright red for *S. commixta*, pink into white for *S. hupehensis* and orange scarlet for *S. sargentiana*. The maples provide foliage spectacle as their leaves turn gold and red, the paperbark maple (*Acer griseum*) being the most spectacular of all.

Shrubs also fruit. Pyracanthas, hollies, cotoneasters and berberis are heavy with berries until the birds make off with them. More arresting are the heps on briar and species roses with arching branches to tempt the flower arranger. And the flower garden has a splendid finale in the form of fuchsias, dahlias and chrysanthemums.

Unlike spring, autumn tints are far more controllable by their very nature for they stick within a sunset palette. Even the strongest of crimsons quickly dissolves into neighbouring oranges and yellows to form an overall harmony. At no other time of the year is the quality of light such a major contributing factor to the achievement of a total effect – savour every precious minute of what is a supreme natural work of art.

WINTER

*

Winter is the ultimate test of good garden design. If your garden is not interesting to look at and wander through from the time the leaves fall until the first flush of spring it must contain faults, and winter is the season in which to rectify them. This is the time to plot, plan and execute alterations and adjustments.

I fully accept that this is the attitude of the gardener as a designer, not as a plantsman. The latter will inevitably regard every major fall of snow and severe frost as a disaster mutilating and killing off precious tender plants. In a bad winter the requiems can be many for lost treasures, but it cannot be denied that there is dazzling beauty in a garden spangled by a sharp frost, or that a well-designed garden under a moderate fall of snow reveals the beauty of its geometry in a way which cannot be matched even in June.

It requires a sophisticated eye to enjoy winter, as its palette is infinitely subtle: matt and glossy greens, grey-greens, brown greens and golden greens. There are also the shapes of deciduous shrubs and trees to contemplate, and the beauty of their bark. Now is the time to fully appreciate your evergreens, not only clipped hedges and conifers but winter-flowering shrubs such as *Viburnum tinus*, and the mahonias. To these might be added other winter delights; *Garrya elliptica* with its grey-green catkins; *Viburnum farreri* (alias *V. fragrans*) and *V. bodnantense*; and witch hazel (*Hamamelis mollis*).

Scattered into this monochrome picture every flower assumes a status which it would never enjoy in the abundance of summer. The hellebores, the Christmas and Lenten roses, are stately blooms with flowers of somewhat surreal colour: green edged with purple, white tinged with purple, even wholly maroon. And no garden is complete without a cluster somewhere of snowdrops which, if the weather is reasonably temperate, appear early in January as harbingers of spring. To these add even the smallest planting of aconites, early crocuses and irises. Remember to plant them lovingly where they will be undisturbed and multiply and where, however tiny your garden, you can annually 'discover' them.

ABOVE Plant structure
disclosed: winter reveals the
subtle beauty of form and
colour of each tree and shrub.
Here the red and yellow
branches of dogwood are
backed by snow.

LEFT The dangerous but
captivating beauty of frost –
clumps of hebes and flowering
grasses are rendered almost
surreal by their icy spangling.

21

'DEAD' BOUNDARIES

*

Boundaries in a garden both enclose and divide. Those constructed of wood, concrete, stone, metal, artificial stone, brick and trellis should be carefully considered in terms of privacy or an element of surprise. They can permanently shut out from vision anything we wish to eliminate, and can equally highlight attractive views beyond the garden by means of gaps or apertures. 'Dead' boundaries can also be 'semi-transparent' screens.

Wood is less utilized than it should be. Two of the most popular wooden boundaries are picket fencing and trellis. The former makes one of the most delightful boundaries for a small front garden, seen at its best in New England. Flowering plants look wonderful tumbling over and through such a fence, which also stands out bright and clean against a clipped hedge.

Both plastic and wooden trellis is available commercially from garden centres, and specialist manufacturers should be able to supply solidly made purpose-built trellis. With imagination, no other inexpensive material can be used so variously, to construct walls, pergolas, arches, gazebos and arbours. It does eventually rot, though its life can be extended with preservative.

Well-designed boundaries made of durable materials involve a heavy capital outlay, but will never be regretted. Walls ensure a sense of enclosure and provide a marvellous background and support for plants.

Hard boundaries within the garden area are also useful. A brick or dry stone retaining wall offers a home for alpine plants, as well as structural support for the level change. To screen one area from another a pierced brick wall can be attractive and many pre-cast pierced concrete blocks are available. For internal boundaries, however, few have more style than balustrading, now available in various lengths of reconstituted stone, with dividing piers. Balustrading forms a splendid containing wall to a terrace, allowing glimpses through to the garden.

Other, minor 'dead' boundaries for flower beds include scallop shells, bricks, edging stone or tiles. They define the bed and look especially attractive if the plants spill over them, breaking the rigid line.

TOP A painted picket fence provides an enchanting boundary to a garden, setting off the plants within and acting as a foil to the dark foliage beyond.

ABOVE Reconstituted stone balustrading makes an elegant architectural boundary to a terrace; here it is softened with a pink climbing rose.

ABOVE Ordinary wattle and picket fencing made delightful by an entanglement of sunflowers and dense summer foliage bursting through.

DEAD BOUNDARIES

1 Reconstituted stone edging
Classical, formal and relatively expensive.

2 Brick edging
Bricks laid diagonally strike an informal note.

3 Dry stone walling
Building a dry stone wall is difficult; if you have one, cherish it.

4 Perforated brick wall
Good for creating internal divisions within a garden, as well as external boundaries.

5 Trellis panelling
White-painted trellis can be used free standing, as shown, to divide space or against walls to give a foothold to climbing plants.

'LIVING' BOUNDARIES

*

'Live' boundaries require vision and patience but, on the bonus side, they are cheaper than 'dead' ones. A living boundary can be a five to ten-year project, even longer if you choose slow-growing plants and envisage a large-scale result. To the novice gardener, hedges seem one of the most boring aspects of garden design: a long rectangular block of greenery slowly reaching the required height. Avoid such a negative approach; on the contrary, hedges are the living backcloth and side wings of the garden scene, and capable of being used creatively. Always draw out how you intend a hedge to grow, and train and trim it from the start with this plan in mind. A hedge is architecture, forming the walls and divisions within a garden, and can be trained to form piers and buttresses, arcades and doorways. As these take shape over the years the hedge becomes progressively more interesting.

In the main it is evergreen hedges which are the most desirable. The one that is planted at the moment *ad nauseam* is the quick-growing Leyland cypress (*Cupressocyparis leylandii*) which I do not despise as much as some do, particularly since the advent of a golden variety, 'Castlewellan'. I would put them ahead of privet (*Ligustrum japonicum*) which is also quick growing but has an insubstantial quality and easily becomes shapeless. The third speedy grower is laurel (*Prunus laurocerasus*) which, with its large shiny leaves, is by far the most interesting. It needs pruning by hand to avoid scarred leaves, and rather more room than the others. Holly (*Ilex aquifolium*) is beautiful because of its glossy leaves and red berries, but the queen of hedges is yew (*Taxus baccata*), and if adequately fed is not as slow growing as books state. No other living boundary adds such distinction to a garden.

Two deciduous hedges are hornbeam (*Carpinus betulus*) and the common beech (*Fagus sylvatica*). Both retain their russet dead leaves through the winter and both, too, can be trained.

Hedges can be delightful given a little thought and imagination. A quite narrow yew hedge about 1.2 metres (4 feet) high with curved 'walls' between linking 'pilas-

BELOW Living boundaries high and low: a yew hedge encloses a strongly geometrical arrangement of beds edged with box and filled with white roses and flowers.

ters' from which arise standard hollies cut into balls or pyramids is a striking garden feature. When it is eventually possible, the top of a hedge can be cut into crenellation, curves or whatever complements the garden composition. 'Windows' can be cut into the 'walls' to frame a view of another part of the garden.

A tapestry hedge is another possibility combining, for example, holly and beech. Where a geometric shape is not necessary, a looser-growing boundary can be made of firethorn (*Pyracantha*), escallonia or barberry (*Berberis*).

Few formal gardens are complete without dwarf hedges. Box (*Buxus sempervirens* 'Suffruticosa') with its unique fragrance and tiny, bright-green leaves is slow growing, but quick-growing santolina, lavender or even rosemary can be used to define and divide a bed into geometric shapes. These low boundaries, in winter, stand revealed as part of the garden's skeleton.

24

LEFT Contrasting hard and soft boundaries in sequence: lavender against a low stone wall with irises and a juniper screen beyond.

ABOVE Instant screening for summer – a cascade of orange and scarlet nasturtiums bring a transitory horticultural triumph to the dullest garden.

HARD
SURFACES

*

The articulation of a garden at ground level depends on hard surfaces. They can define layout and shape, as paths and steps linking one part of the garden to another and as areas designed as focal points or places to sit. In a small garden careful consideration must be given to hard surfaces at the planning stage more than in a large one; the smaller the cultivated area the more likely it is to contain a substantial proportion of hard surface and there is less room to experiment and improvize. Whatever the size of the garden, a mistake in planting can be rectified, but one in paving is very costly to put right. Always look first at your house and choose paving colours and materials sympathetic to it. Never purchase large quantities of paving without trying specimen samples out to see how they look on site; what may look dire in a builder's yard may look surprisingly correct *in situ*, and vice versa. Never make a hurried decision; it is better to make do with a gravel path until the path 'proper' is affordable.

A wooden loggia with raked gravel beneath.

It is important, especially in a small space, not to use too many different materials, or the effect will be fussy and restless. In terms of design, choosing paving can be a depressing experience because reconstituted stone types are so rarely acceptable either in colour or texture. They often come in appalling shades of pink, rust, yellow and green, simulating very badly – if at all – a variety of natural materials. There is a huge gap between these synthetic products and what they purport to represent. Look hard at the range available, then choose the least offensive and most innocuously coloured one.

Stone is considered by many to be the most beautiful of all materials for garden paving, but it is virtually ruled out on grounds of cost. For a small garden, there is little to rival the versatility of brick, though it, too, is relatively expensive. Brick's small scale makes it a perfect surface for limited areas, as does its adaptability. Patterns of brick paving are easy and pleasing to work out on graph paper. The combinations are endless, like variations in basket-weaving, as the bricks are laid diagonally or on their side. There are many traditional patterns which can be expanded or contracted according to the space available. Bricks can be made to fan out into curves and circles or gradually change level or direction. Be careful, however, that the brick you buy is frost resistant or else it will absorb water, freeze and crumble. There are special brick pavers, which are generally thinner and with a larger surface area than normal bricks. They are not necessarily better value than an ordinary frost-proof facing brick, provided it is well chosen.

As with bricks, cobbles can be arranged in any number of geometric patterns. The cheapest natural material of all must be gravel, which has been used in every great garden since the Renaissance. In these days, it is not difficult to keep these surfaces weed free with the aid of modern weedkillers.

As a natural material, wood looks absolutely right in an informal garden setting, either as a path made of the discs of a tree trunk, or as railway sleepers laid side by side. It is not a sensible surface material for damp climates, though, as it becomes slippery underfoot and quickly rots.

A great deal of garden design depends on successful cheating through visual deception. Paving is a huge expense, far in excess of any of the plants; often it is a matter of marrying natural and synthetic paving in the right way. The effect of huge tracks of concrete slabs can be negated by introducing areas of brick or cobble, making sure that these occur at focal points, such as a flight of steps or at the base of a statue or a sundial. Gaps between the slabs can be filled with sprawling plants.

BELOW Irregular shaped setts, arranged in formal concentric circles outwards from the garden's focal point, with box topiary and a herbaceous border behind.

ABOVE An interesting path in an informal garden, slices of tree trunk wend their way through ferns and grasses.

HARD SURFACES

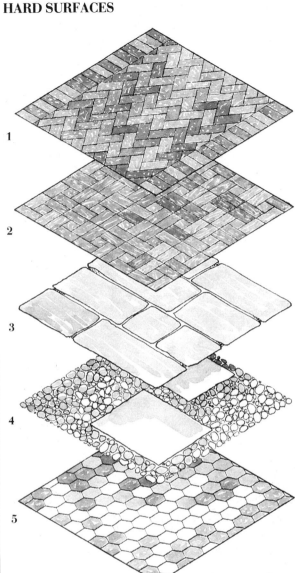

1 **Brick paving** laid in a herringbone pattern with single brick edging: pretty but very expensive.

2 **Brick paving** laid in a variation of the basket-weave pattern: costly, but timeless and maintenance free.

3 **York stone paving** is larger scale than brick but, like it, very expensive and a life-time investment.

4 **Cobbles and stone,** or reconstituted stone, make a pretty combination; the cobbles are not for walking on.

5 **Quarry tiles,** in an unusual hexagonal pattern, give a harder feel than brick and stone; rectangular tiles are more common.

SOFT
SURFACES

*

The association of almost any form of garden with grass is a relatively recent one, stemming largely from the English landscape tradition of the great parks in the eighteenth century with their rolling acres of lawn dotted with clumps of trees. Placed into that perspective, it can be seen how very inappropriate grass is for small and, in particular, very small gardens. These vestigial pocket handkerchiefs not only look absurd but need year-round maintenance, which can be as intensive as that required to produce whole borders of shrubs and flowers.

Grass, therefore, is only for the largest of small gardens where it can be deployed on a scale which reads correctly as a restful verdant colour and a texture which responds well to variations in light; as the ideal link between flower beds and paths; as natural underplanting for small trees and shrubs and as an area on which the family can sit. There are a great many types of grass and grass mixtures and it is essential to choose the one which is suitable for your climate and garden. Never underestimate the work a lawn involves. It has to be regularly mown throughout the growing season; the edges have to be clipped and kept in trim; and the lawn-mower has to be housed and, during the winter months, annually serviced. In a larger garden it may be possible to close cut only part of the grass, letting the rest grow taller. Wild flowers could be grown in the long grass but even that would have to be cut down at least twice in a season. Remember that the mowings have to be put somewhere and that there are few sights more depressing than a lawn lacking water. Unless a lawn is kept regularly watered in dry weather it quickly turns to a deadly straw colour.

On the positive side, no other plant takes treading upon as kindly as grass. Others may bear occasional incursions from human feet but in general they do not like it. Chamomile (*Anthemis nobilis*) is one of them, and so are varieties of thyme (*Thymus serpyllum*). One of the gardens (page 54) makes use of baby's tears (*Helxine soleirolii*) to stunning effect but it is not for walking across. Various periwinkles, ivies and moss produce the same effect, but stepping stones are needed.

ABOVE Wood bark chippings form a meandering walkway, responding to the asymmetrical planting of the flowers and shrubs.

RIGHT A sophisticated contrast in texture: a carpet of baby's tears encircles clipped box, with grass beyond.

SEATING

*

The seat is an integral part of a garden. It expresses the basic philosophy of the garden, as a place for contemplation and pleasure. From classical antiquity down through the Renaissance to modern times men and women have sat in their gardens to enjoy the beauty of the fragrance, the bloom, the ever-changing colour of the seasons. And, above all in the small garden, to survey with pride the fruits of their own labours.

I wish to make one point about folding chairs and deck-chairs; always choose those with materials and patterns in predominantly neutral shades of brown or green. Garden upholstery in violently coloured fabrics spattered with gargantuan floral patterns is a monument to tastelessness. Visitors are forced to look at the furniture and not the flowers, and people look absolutely awful sitting on them. When contemplating buying such seating, make sure you have somewhere handy to store it out of season.

There are two more categories of seating: movable and immovable. The latter is usually of cast iron, stone or reconstituted stone. Antique cast iron and stone garden benches can, of course, be acquired but at a premium. Fortunately, there is a wide range of reproduction benches and seats on the market in both materials. Reconstituted stone benches, straight or curved, come in classic patterns derived from seventeenth- and eighteenth-century prototypes. They are garden classics, require no maintenance and eventually develop a patina. The modern equivalent of cast iron seats, however, require painting from time to time to avert rust.

Seats can be dominant objects and their style should relate to the garden's style. A seat, for example, in the

BELOW Cane seats and a wooden table and bench make a summer outdoor dining room behind a hollyhock screen.

RIGHT Solitary splendour: a single, elegant, comfortable wooden seat is placed to enjoy a vista; in turn, the seat becomes a focal point.

ABOVE A reconstituted stone bench of classic design, surrounded by herbs.

SEATING

1 Reproduction Gothick garden seat in white-painted aluminium alloy.
2 Victorian park bench in natural slatted wood and iron.
3 Reproduction Lutyens bench in white-painted wood.
4 Classic wooden bench in untreated oak.

grand manner of Sir Edwin Lutyens would look totally out of place in a cottage garden. There should be no problem about purchasing well-designed wooden seats; fortunately, the most basic wooden teak seat with arms and a slatted back almost defies bastardization. Wooden seats can look equally good in natural wood, especially when the colour is tempered by time, or painted in colours sympathetic to the garden scene. Peeling paint is never attractive, and if you commit yourself to painted woodwork, you are also committed to regular sanding and repainting.

For the inventive, the possibilities for devizing seating are endless and that is where the fun begins. A section of a tree trunk makes a splendid solitary seat provided it is stable, and level. Piers of stone or brick supporting a wooden railway sleeper or thick wooden plank make an equally good one. Large concrete paving stones can be used in exactly the same way, and any flight of steps or indeed any change of level can provide an *ad hoc* seat.

Most important of all, seats can be framed within a setting. Even the most rudimentary seat can be trans- formed into a magical bower by coaxing a prolific rose, clematis or honeysuckle over a surrounding pergola. An elementary wooden structure covered in trellis built around a seat makes a charming gazebo. A clipped evergreen hedge surrounding a seat like a pair of brackets gives it a dignified architectural framework as well as shelter from winds and sun.

Siting a permanent garden seat requires careful plan- ning. The view, the need for protection from the elements, and exposure to the sun should influence the positioning. Permanent garden seats should sensibly stand on a hard surface. There is nothing so maddening as placing a seat on grass and having to hand clip round it every time you mow. The grass underneath is bound to suffer from the shade in any case.

Is the seat for a momentary pause or is it for an afternoon's read in the open? For the former the simplest bench will suffice, for the latter, a comfortable seat capable of taking a few cushions is better, and more conducive\ to restful sojourns. If the ground nearby is level, to take a small table or cool drink, so much the better.

In a small garden the best way to approach the problem of seating is to have an immovable one with auxiliary seating stored within easy reach. The latter can be brought out and utilized as necessary; for weekend guests or impromptu parties outdoors. A small garden dotted with permanent seats is best avoided, as it has vague amusement-park overtones.

32

ABOVE Ordinary paving slabs set slightly above ground level make an ingenious inexpensive bench. The sprays of yellow broom and stones visually off-set the slabs' hardness.

RIGHT An inventive garden sofa, made of an old tree trunk placed on top of two stone supports, and cushioned by clipped box.

ARCHES AND PERGOLAS

*

Much of garden architecture is transitory, in particular wooden supports for climbing plants (occasionally brick, stone or iron is used but these are expensive). The great thing about transitory garden architecture is that the most spectacular effects can be attained with the cheapest of materials used with ingenuity. However, even with proper preparation and preservatives, the life of such structures is inevitably finite; within a decade it will need renewing.

Nonetheless, let your imagination – which can be fired by other people's gardens, books and magazines – be fired to create plant supports, screens, arches, corridors and architectural meeting points.

While there is room in a large garden to experiment with a wide range of styles and materials, small gardens should relate closely to the architecture of the house. If your house is modern, extend the clean lines of its composition into the garden, using precise geometric shapes without decorative detail or excrescences. A country cottage betokens rustic pergola work forming arches, screens and bowers through which roses, clematis and honeysuckle tumble. A town house in the classical style requires formal structures in trellis constructed in symmetrical ordered shapes.

In a small area these structures can act as focal points, divide the garden to create the illusion of space, or provide entrances, exits and corridors. Arches are perhaps one of the most beguiling forms of garden architecture. A single arch covered with climbing plants can act as a frame through which one passes into the magic of the garden. A series can form a passage or pergola. Make them wide enough for easy passage and high enough so that one's hat or hair is not caught in the branches.

Think of these structures not merely as plant supports but as picture frames leading the eye on to whatever is framed. Like hedges, arches and pergolas control the way we look at space in the garden. Such structures should be considered at the planning stage, when it might be appropriate to make a scale model in cardboard with a tiny cut-out human figure. By experimenting at this stage you can avoid large-scale mistakes.

ABOVE An expensive but beautiful stone and brick arch acts as a frame to the garden beyond and supports a climbing rose.

ABOVE RIGHT A simple painted wooden pergola bearing a luxuriant canopy of wisteria.

ABOVE FAR RIGHT An elegant rose-covered iron arbour is further enhanced by the evergreen backdrop.

ARCHES AND PERGOLAS

1 Wooden poles and rope are ideal for training rose garlands.
2 Wire mesh arbour makes a plant-covered focal point.

3 Wooden pergola on brick piers is a more permanent feature.
4 Iron trellis adds an old-fashioned touch.

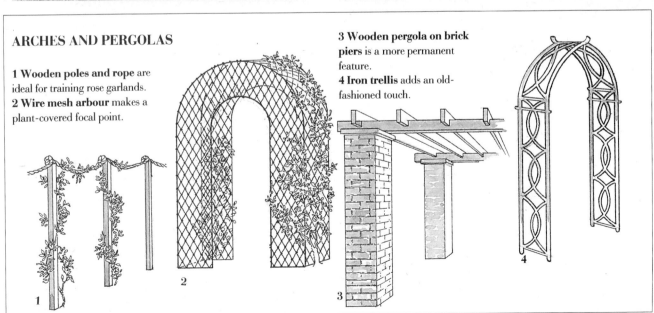

1

2

3

4

35

TRAINING

*

Training is the imposition on to plants of order and pattern, usually of a highly geometric or architectural character. For the novice gardener it is one of the most difficult things with which to come to terms, for training requires time. Everything in our age is geared to the instant, so that the notion of having to wait between five and ten years to achieve an effect seems too demanding. It is therefore foolish to embark on a garden which depends on training for its composition, if the intention is not to occupy the house for more than a decade. The second point is that plants actually grow faster than is recognized (a photographic record will prove the point) and with good stock and tending, most effects are well on their way in five years. It is the first two of these which seem agonizingly slow.

Bold architectural shapes in yew (*Taxus baccata*) or box (*Buxus sempervirens*) add class to a garden, whether formal or cottage-garden style. With modern mechanical clipping, topiary has very much come back into fashion. Topiary in box can be bought ready trained but at vast expense, though I prefer yew. In a small garden one clipped yew tapered cone topped by a topiary bird makes a splendid focal point. Other shrubs, particularly holly (*Ilex*), bay (*Laurus nobilis*), or the common hawthorn (*Crataegus*), can be clipped into shape, but not as precisely as yew and box.

A small garden has only a limited space for trees and one which can be close planted, trained and pruned is the red-twigged lime (*Tilia platyphyllos* 'Rubra'). In quite a small area an elegant lime walk can be made by pleaching: bending and intertwining the shoots along a frame of wood or bamboo. Fruit trees on dwarf rooting stock can be grown in a small space, trained as espaliers, cordons and fans, against a wall, or as specimens.

Formally trained plants are important to garden design, and take on special emphasis in winter, when more transient colour is absent. Branches pruned into an architectural framework, and evergreens cut into shapes, are part of the permanent abstract pattern which makes any garden in winter still beautiful to look at.

1

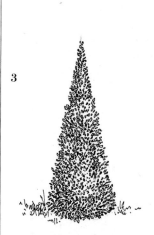

2

3

4

1 Double horizontal cordon-trained fruit trees can be grown against a wall or free standing, to form a living fence.
2 Fan-trained fruit trees are best grown against a wall; Morello cherries and peaches are a suitable subject for training in this way.

3 A formal topiary cone of yew or box, or, more unusually, of clipped bay or holly.
4 A double-leader summer jasmine trained up a pole to eventually cover a wire globe.

RIGHT Here, low box hedging, punctuated by box topiary clipped into ball shapes, gives a sinuous edge to a rose bed.

BELOW The abstract shapes of pollarded limes bursting into leaf resemble extraordinary natural candelabras.

WATER

*

To successfully use water in a small space, very careful thought and design are required; of all garden ingredients, this is the one which can most easily look ridiculous. Few things are more depressing in the average small garden than the so-called natural pools. They are almost without exception a terrible mistake and the blame lies with the mass proliferation of instant plastic pools sold by garden centres. On the whole, plastic pools provide little more than entertainment centres for the local cats.

Some of the most successful examples of the use of water in a garden are those which give virtually the whole area available to water, or are so designed to create that illusion. The effect is that of a true water garden and not a garden into which a ludicrous puddle of water has been added. The artificial pond is a simple geometric sheet of water which makes no attempt to imitate nature.

A water garden requires constant attention: a passing heron can devour fish, if there are any; unless the water is kept clean and aerated it can quickly become stagnant and smell. Drought can present appalling problems as water evaporates; the lining can spring a leak and you can awaken to an empty crater. Unless protected with netting, in the autumn, dead leaves fall into the water and foul it; in winter the surface can become a block of ice, making life hard for the fish, and possibly damaging the structure of the pool. However, these disadvantages must be set against the undeniable beauty of a large, well-maintained pond, set beneath a clear sunny sky.

Smaller water elements can be attractive in their own way, and if they contain no plants or fish, are easier to cope with. A dolphin or lion's head mask or even a simple pipe set into a wall spouting water into a bowl, cistern or trough provide the imagery of water without actually requiring enormous commitment, and can make an attractive focal point for a town garden or the termination of a vista. Around it can be built a tableau of plants such as irises or hostas. More elaborate fountains should be approached with extreme caution and would be out of place in a constricted space, where utter simplicity of treatment must be the rule.

LEFT A small quantity of water can be used to great effect. Here a simple water spout is enhanced by a still life of pottery behind it.

BELOW A garden given over almost entirely to water with a decking walk way.

BOTTOM An asymmetrical treatment of a circular pool filled with lilies and grasses and framed by hedging.

ORNAMENTS

*

Garden ornaments should not be an afterthought or an unnecessary elaboration – if they are to be used at all they should be considered from the outset of garden planning. Leaves wither, flowers bloom and fade but garden ornaments occupy space twelve months of the year.

For those who can afford antiques, there are specialist dealers selling every form of garden ornament and decoration.

Good reproduction sculpture does exist. The best is sold with a specific reference that it is a facsimile of an original and gives the location of the source. These items are expensive but often very handsome. Odd pieces of architectural sculpture can sometimes be picked up from demolition sites or junk shops. But, for the majority, choice is limited to what is available commercially. Be wary of ornamental figures. Stick instead to simple forms and shapes: obelisks, balls and pineapples. Even these can be bastardized, so if you feel uncertain, seek the advice of a friend with a feeling for such things.

Small gardens usually require only one ornament, and any multiplication leads to a result akin to a churchyard. That one ornament will almost invariably be the focal point, and will be exposed to detailed examination because there is no space for indulging in the optical tricks possible when the viewer is prevented from getting close to the object. Make that ornament an investment; spend on it as much as you would for a major kitchen appliance: unlike the latter, the ornament does not need replacing.

Two ornaments in a restricted area should be a pair, such as two obelisks, flanking a seat. Scale is all-important. Small ornaments can be placed on a plinth to add importance and height; excessively large ornaments look ridiculous. Cut out the shape in cardboard first and try it in the garden. Do not be surprised if an ornament eventually ends up elsewhere; it often takes a couple of years for the composition to fall in place.

Avoid any poor-quality or unnaturally coloured ornament with colour wash simulating 'dirt' in the crevices. One of the joys of gardening is watching ornaments age, a process which can be hastened by pouring over sour milk.

A single stone ball adds a simple architectural shape to balance the informality of a roughly built stone wall and tumbling rock roses.

ORNAMENTS

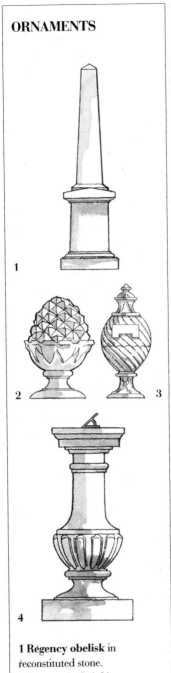

1 Regency obelisk in reconstituted stone.
2 Pineapple finial in reconstituted stone.
3 Alexander Pope's urn in reconstituted stone.
4 Sundial on reconstituted stone plinth.

ABOVE This large terracotta pot is visually strong enough to remain empty; a handsome focal point to a garden.

LEFT A stone basket of fruit provides a charming classical element.

CONTAINERS

*

Before I embark on the delights of containers let me dwell on their drawbacks. They require work, and anyone who wishes to garden with the minimum of effort should forgo them. The only maintenance-free plants I know for container growing are stonecrops or *Sempervivum*. Mound up the soil high and tuck in several varieties; these multiply and eventually cascade over the edges. Apart from stonecrops, plants in containers require regular servicing: replacing compost, feeding and watering. Container gardening calls for a commitment – few things are more depressing than one awash in weeds or bearing a trophy of dead blooms.

On the positive side, containers present a mass of opportunities. One general point needs, however, to be stressed: although plain plastic pots can be successful indoors they should be avoided outside. As in the case of ornaments, containers in a natural environment should

BELOW An unusual and effective tableau of plants in contemporary containers and stones of varying sizes.

ABOVE Summer signals the evacuation of plants from house to garden. In this instance, terracotta pots of scarlet pelargoniums complement the paving.

42

CONTAINERS

1 **Basketweave pot** in
reconstituted stone.
2 **Terracotta pot** with garlands.
3 **Versailles tub** in white-
painted wood.
4 **Classical urn** in reconstituted
stone.
5 **Half beer barrel** wooden tub.

ideally be made of natural materials: stone, lead, wood, clay, terracotta or reconstituted stone. The only exceptions are painted wooden tubs or painted fibreglass to pass as wood and lead.

If you have space and enough light the movable containers – whether clay, stone or reconstituted stone – can be stored indoors over the winter. Larger pots – troughs, urns, tubs and jardinieres – form part of the immovable features of the garden and it is better to have one good one than a plethora of bad. There is a wide selection of well-designed containers available, both contemporary and old. Terracotta pots, either plain or with a moulding in the form of swags or lions' heads, are classics. Those manufactured and exported from Italy are by far the best. There are some very badly designed and made terracotta pots also, which can be recognized by poor shape and line, and crudity of decoration.

Tubs have great style. The wooden half barrel, available in several sizes, secured by metal hoops is a more homely version of the elegant Versailles tub which, painted white and sporting a bay or box tree clipped as an obelisk or ball, has undeniable chic.

There are a large number of reproduction containers with style, often exact copies of those in the greatest gardens. The classical urn on a pedestal can rarely be equalled, although a stone basket comes near to it as a vehicle for displaying flowering plants. And, as in the case of an ornament, scale and positioning of containers are all important.

Containers are wonderful vehicles for instant changes of mood and effect. I love filling urns with hyacinths which bring spring up to eye level when seen from my house. There is that magical day in early summer when it is warm enough to put pots of geraniums out, transforming in a trice the whole look of the garden. Containers can be filled with plants virtually in flower, purchased from a nursery, to bring instant colour to the dullest enclosure. But do provide adequate drainage in the bottom and good potting compost, and water and feed regularly or all your efforts will be pointless.

INDULGENCES

*

Follies dot the great gardens of the world in every shape and form, from a Chinese pagoda to a triumphal arch, from a fake ruined castle to a hermitage. The folly makes an important point for every garden stylist: the garden has always been a place in which to express indulgence, to build a private dreamworld in which to muse.

This role is just as valid for the smallest of gardens; those described in this book offer an alternative series of private Arcadias. In your own garden, let your fancy roam free, and your indulgences heighten your garden as an expression of yourself and your family. A romantic rose garden could be 'peopled' by cut-out figures from another age. A sculptor could be commissioned to make a column or an obelisk inscribed with family initials or the date of a wedding or birth of a child. Monumental inscriptions are not just for the graveyard – an inscription inset, for example, into the walls of a garden could celebrate an event or bear a line of verse to reinforce the mood you wish to evoke by the planting.

Into the category of extravagant indulgences I would place good old statues and urns, the use of real stone and any form of garden building, be it temple, grotto, summer house or swimming pool. All involve heavy outlay and some involve the use of contractors, even possibly designers and architects. Always remember the tradition that garden buildings are not meant only to be utilitarian but works of the imagination, drawing on every conceivable historical style. That element of imagination has been lost in this century, eliminated by firms which manufacture wooden summer houses like huts for chickens. A fretwork gothick arbour or a summer house with turrets and crenellation has enchantment and wit – now is the time to revive them.

Topiary, too, offers endless possibilities. Everything from a house to a series of chessmen, even letters of the alphabet, can be formed by clipping. Such things give a garden indisputable character and uniqueness. Whatever style you choose, use indulgences to break through the conformity which has made the average modern garden a monotonous variant of a few well-worn clichés.

BELOW A full-size 'confessional' in *Thuya* strikes an eccentric note in a formal garden.

BOTTOM This Muse of Music *trompe l'oeil* cut-out figure makes a witty movable substitute for sculpture.

RIGHT An otherwise ordinary garden is given a touch of fantasy by the presence of a Victorian dovecote.

The
DREAM
GARDENS

*

The twenty-four gardens that follow have been chosen for their very real and individual sense of style. They are not only an expression of a particular owner or designer, but a response to circumstances, architecture, use and location. Each of the stunningly successful designs is a 'recipe' but none needs to be – nor, indeed, could be – followed slavishly.

The planting plans that accompany the illustrations represent, as accurately as possible, the original schemes. There is a certain amount of artistic licence, sometimes because the original plans were unavailable or never existed, other times because the planting, as it developed, changed markedly from the original scheme. In every case, the suggested alternative planting has been chosen to be empathetic to the character and personality of the particular garden.

The
SECLUDED
GARDEN

*

This garden shows what can be done in the type of space found at the back of nineteenth-century town houses – a small rectangle enclosed by a brick wall. In this instance, there is space on one side of the house, too, making an L-shape. The garden is so small that the approach has been to think of it as a *tableau* seen from the house, treating the area rather like a conservatory or greenhouse devoid of glazing. The main vista resembles exactly the lush exuberance of an Edwardian conservatory, with its abundance of palms and potted plants. The modern deck chair strikes the only discordant note – I would have chosen real or reproduction nineteenth-century iron furniture.

Everything here is seen at such close range that there is no room for cheap materials. The owner started with the advantage of good old brick walls but matching bricks have been found to outline the small pool, and the York-stone paving is of good quality. The statue which completes the vista must bear close scrutiny too, whereas in large gardens poor ornaments can be disguised simply by means of distance.

There is an insistence on straight lines, defining the planting beds that run parallel to the boundary walls and along the side of the house. The dense effect is created by over-planting and the generous use of plants in containers. Of course, the palms would have to be brought indoors during the winter, and so would most of the other potted plants. Containerized plants are high-maintenance objects – like the cat sitting on the wall, one cannot go away and leave them.

Evergreens hide the end wall, providing a leafy bower for the statue and a gentle intimation that, perhaps, the garden extends further than it really does. The main effect comes from a splendid trio. New Zealand flax (*Phormium tenax*) has huge, sword-shaped leaves and makes a pleasing contrast to the hand-shaped leaves of *Fatsia japonica*, a shelter-loving plant that has branching panicles of white flowers in early autumn. The third evergreen, the lovely *Magnolia grandiflora*, is more suitable for the walls of a large country house; in smaller gardens, it must be pruned fairly radically every few

A panorama from the first floor shows the basic geometric plan of the garden, overlaid with rich and varied planting. The light-reflecting pool contributes to the effect, and the statue adds a feeling of timeless elegance and repose to the secluded urban garden scene.

years. A variety of *Pyracantha* or evergreen honeysuckle might be more appropriate.

There are a variety of trees tucked into this minute area, all different in foliage shape and colour, bark and branch formation: two Japanese maples – *Acer palmatum* 'Dissectum' with its finely cut leaves and the purple-tinged *A.p.* 'Atropurpureum' – a golden-leaved *Robinia pseudoacacia* 'Frisia' and a sycamore. The latter tree, however, could quickly outgrow and overpower the area.

A mass of other plants have been crammed in too: jasmine, tobacco plants, white busy Lizzies, roses, clematis, tree peonies, camellias, yellow-green lady's mantle, fuchsias, the common hop (*Humulus lupulus*) and ferns. This is a wonderful garden, but it requires keen, year-round cultivation. The reward, though, is visual satisfaction on a spectacular scale.

KEY TO PLAN

1. *Hedera helix* 'Hibernica'
2. *Robinia pseudoacacia* 'Frisia'
3. *Fatsia japonica*
4. *Clematis* hybrid
5. *Phormium tenax*
6. *Magnolia grandiflora*
7. *Camellia japonica* 'Mercury'
8. *Vitis coignetiae*
9. *Pittosporum tobira*
10. *Acer palmatum* 'Osakazuki'
11. *Impatiens wallerana*
12. *Nicotiana affinis (N. alata)*
13. *Eucalyptus gunnii*
14. *Clematis armandii*
15. *Betula pendula*
16. *Hedera canariensis* 'Gloire de Marengo'
17. *Prunus subhirtella* 'Autumnalis Alba'
18. *Parthenocissus veitchii*
19. *Rosa* 'Cardinal de Richelieu'
20. *Daphne* × *burkwoodii*
21. *Camellia* × *williamsii* 'Bow Bells'
22. *Acer palmatum* 'Atropurpureum'
23. *Chamaerops excelsa* (syn. *Trachycarpus fortunei*)
24. *Arundinaria* sp.
25. *Paeonia lutea*
26. *Humulus lupulus* 'Aureus'
27. *Acer palmatum* 'Dissectum'
28. *Fuschia* hybrid
29. *Leptospermum* sp.
30. *Hosta* sp.

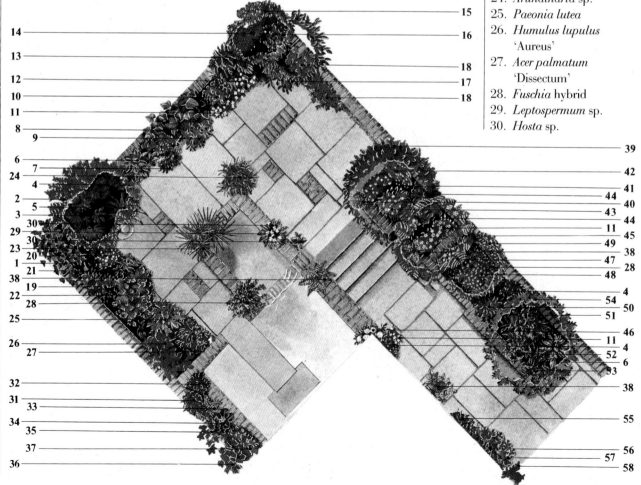

31. *Clematis montana* 'Alba'
32. *Camellia japonica* 'Mathotiana Alba'
33. *Athyrium filix-femina*
34. *Bergenia* hybrid
35. × *Fatshedera lizei*
36. *Vitis vinifera* 'Madeleine Angevine'
37. *Acer palmatum* 'Senkaki'
38. *Osmunda regalis*
39. *Malus* 'Veitch's Scarlet'
40. *Lavandula spica* 'Hidcote'
41. *Convolvulus cneorum*
42. *Jaminum nudiflorum*
43. *Fothergilla monticola*
44. *Fremontodendron californicum*
45. *Acacia dealbata*
46. *Rosa* 'New Dawn'
47. *Abelia* 'Francis Mason'
48. *Ceratostigma willmottianum*
49. *Betula pendula* 'Youngii'
50. *Camellia japonica* 'Elegans'
51. *Rhododendron* 'Unique'
52. *Pachysandra terminalis*
53. *Abelia chinensis* 'Albovariegata'
54. *Acer platanoides* 'Crimson King'
55. *Jasminum officinale*
56. *Hedera helix* 'Goldheart'
57. *Alchemilla mollis*
58. *Wisteria floribunda* var.

French windows frame the view of the main vista, with the statue as the focal point. Though many of the plants are perfectly hardy, the effect in summer is one of tropical profusion.

The
COLOUR-THEME GARDEN

*

Colour control in a garden is everything. The high priestess of that control was Gertrude Jekyll, whose book *Colour Schemes for the Flower Garden*, first published in 1908, remains an enduring classic and inspiration. Her approach is never doctrinaire and she begins her discussion of gardens using one or two colours with this warning:

> '. . . a blue garden, for beauty's sake, may be hungering for lemon yellow, but it is not allowed to have it because it is called the blue garden, and there must be no flowers in it but blue flowers. I can see no sense in this . . . any experienced colourist knows that the blues will be more telling – more purely blue – by the juxtaposition of rightly placed complementary colour.'

She then proceeds to provide a plan for a sequence of colour gardens, moving the eye through orange into grey, gold, blue and green. One rule overrides every other: the avoidance of clash or stridency even within the range of a single colour.

To limit a small garden to only one colour, say white or grey, could, I believe, be monotonous and boring. Single-colour designs are safer when they are one part of the very large garden that has room for such indulgences. In a small space it would be difficult to achieve interest and enough variety with less than two colours. In this garden there is a classic combination of purple-blue and yellow flowers, but, following the Jekyll advice to break rules, flecks of magenta and white are incorporated. In such a restricted area pink and white, orange and grey or blue and white could be equally successful, but you should avoid any of the very hot and strong reds. I cannot give better advice than that your approach should be painterly, and indeed Impressionist paintings offer an ideal point of reference for this type of subtle orchestration of colour.

Very careful planning must go into a garden of this kind not only to attain balance of composition but to ensure interest across the seasons. The illustration is of the garden in summer with the yellows made up, for example, of day lilies (*Hemerocallis*), lady's mantle (*Alchemilla mollis*) and yarrow (*Achillea*). Other yellow alternatives would be the daisy-like ox-eye chamomile (*Anthemis tinctoria*), golden rod (*Solidago* × *hybrida*) or coreopsis. The purple-blues of knapweed (*Centaurea*), sage (*Salvia*) and garden pansies (*Viola* × *wittrockiana*) in this garden could equally be provided by campanulas, Russell lupins (*Lupinus* hybrids) or one of the violet-blue border phlox, such as 'Harlequin' or 'Marlborough'. Here, touches of white come from delphiniums, *Lychnis* and *Achillea ptarmica*; but white peonies or white agapanthus are pretty alternatives. For spring and autumn interest in the case of the blues there should be crocuses, scillas, grape hyacinths and a whole range of asters; for the yellows, crocuses again running through to heleniums. Many books and nursery catalogues list plants under colour and season so that you may make your own choice. More important is the fact that colour-restricted gardens need a background such as a hedge or wall, to set off the effect to advantage. Seen against a hectic multicoloured background, a colour-restricted garden becomes fairly meaningless. My own inclinations in a small garden would be to confine such colour essays to a single area or border rather than deny myself so much. Alternatively, one could change colours with the seasons: a blue and white spring garden becoming an orange and grey summer one. Masterly orchestration is called for.

A small garden planted as though by an Impressionist painter with a classic combination of purple-blue and yellow flowers with very occasional touches of magenta and white.

The
CARPET
GARDEN

*

Shade need not be the gardener's enemy. It is only when shade is combined with dry poor soil – under greedy trees, for example – that plants find it difficult to survive. If the soil is enriched with well-rotted organic matter and regularly watered, there is no limit to the lush effects that can be achieved. Here, in a tiny courtyard behind a nineteenth-century town house, shade has been totally defeated. The area is irregular in shape and virtually sunless with towering walls on all sides. These walls have been painted white – an important point, for they reflect any available light and offset the greenery. Red brick walls would be sombre and would reflect little light.

The single, large raised planting bed is surrounded by gravel, which extends up to the walls of the house. The inspiration for the planting is twofold: the vegetation typically found at the bottom of a deep ravine, and the famous Japanese moss gardens of Kyoto and Nara.

Here, in this French garden, the velvet of moss is replaced with *Helxine soleirolii*, more correctly *Soleirolia soleirolii*, and, more popularly, mind-your-own-business or baby's tears. It is moderately hardy, and evergreen in mild winters, but has the disadvantage that if it is exposed to frost, the leaves turn black. It is a rampant relative of the stinging nettle and, like it, can be a real nuisance, especially in the rock garden or greenhouse. Here, the gravel surrounding the raised bed can be sprayed with weedkiller to prevent unwanted colonies becoming established. Almost the same effect could be achieved by using small-leaved ivies, or periwinkle (*Vinca minor*) which has pretty flowers from late spring to midsummer. All of these plants need a soil enriched with well-rotted manure, garden compost or leaf mould.

The Japanese angelica tree (*Aralia elata*) introduces an element of height to the garden. Its huge pinnate leaves are deciduous, so that, in winter, the architectural form of its pale, spiny stems is visible. The Mexican orange (*Choisya ternata*) provides an evergreen backdrop with its shiny leaves, while the white feathery panicles of plume poppy (*Macleaya cordata*) reach a height of 3 ft (90 cm) or more in summer.

Other herbaceous perennials poking through the carpet of *Helxine* include Japanese anemone (*Anemone hupehensis*) with its cup-shaped pink or white flowers, Siberian bugloss (*Brunnera macrophylla*), which boasts heart-shaped leaves and a springtime display of tiny, blue forget-me-not flowers, and spotted dead nettle (*Lamium maculatum* 'Roseum'). The nettle adds just the right amount of variegation and its summer flowers are a clear pink, not the insipid mauve characteristic of the species.

The deeply divided leaves of *Helleborus foetidus* are like long green fingers; here they form a thick, dark clump contrasting with the dainty, bright dead nettle. I would include as many varieties of these beautiful flowers as I could – for example, the pretty Christmas rose (*H. niger*) or Lenten rose (*H. orientalis*). They are long-lived, tolerant plants, flowering over many weeks in winter or spring. Those of the stinking hellebore are small green, maroon-edged bells. Other species and cultivars range in colour from the pure white of *H.n.* 'Potter's Wheel', to the deep, purple-black blossoms of the Lenten rose hybrid 'Heartsease'.

Ivy is used for the wall-covering here, but I might choose the self-clinging climbing hydrangea (*Hydrangea anomala petiolaris*) instead. In large areas of sun or shade, it makes an equally good ground cover, clothing the soil with round, fresh green leaves, and flat, greeny-white flowers in midsummer.

This is a most unusual town garden, deliberately eschewing any formal architectural arrangement. The addition of a central urn or statue would provide a year-round focal point without, I think, losing that quality. Maintenance is, on the whole, minimal – the final result is utterly charming.

General view of the shady courtyard. Notice the total colour control – a palette of greens with a very few white or pink flowers providing occasional flecks of colour.

KEY TO PLAN

1. *Hedera helix*
2. *Ailanthus altissima*
3. *Ficus carica*
4. *Fatsia japonica*
5. *Aralia elata*
6. *Choisya ternata*
7. *Dryopteris filix-mas*
8. *Macleaya cordata*
9. *Helleborus foetidus*
10. *Lamium maculatum* 'Roseum'
11. *Luzula nivea*
12. *Brunnera macrophylla*
13. *Anemone hupehensis*
14. *Campanula portenschlagiana*
15. *Helxine soleirolii*

The cascading leaves of the *Aralia elata* shelter ferns and flowers which include *Helleborus foetidus* and *Lamium maculatum* 'Roseum'.

A detail of baby's tears ground cover and *Brunnera macrophylla*, which has blue, forget-me-not summer flowers.

The
CORRIDOR HERB
GARDEN

*

There are two sorts of herb garden: the formal and the cottage. The latter depends on an artful cascade of plants arranged in proximity to the kitchen door. But in this herb garden, splendidly Italianate in feeling, meticulous attention has been paid to every detail: the juxtaposition of hard surface materials, of leaf shapes, of plant forms, of colours and of scents.

Here, a virtue has been made out of what is an awkward shape, a narrow rectangle. Its length has been emphasized by the walls of evergreen yew which provide protection for shelter-loving herbs and make a successful play on perspective. In the distance, at the end of the path, the hedge has been deliberately cut lower to form an architectural wall, decorated in the centre like gate piers with balls on the top, giving glimpses of a distant view beyond.

The key to the design, however, is the break half-way along the brick-edged gravel path where, with an old millstone as a focal point, circles of stone, brick and gravel provide a centre to the garden. This is reinforced by the clipped domes of golden box, four at the centre and two at the entrance, and the green box spirals that provide a perfect architectural framework to set off the herbs. I confess that I would want to place stone seats on either side of the central circle to savour to the full the beauty and fragrance of the herbs. But there are delights enough here to inspire anyone to embark on a formal herb garden, however modest in scale.

The introduction of the golden box is perhaps the master touch, off-setting the greens and greys. The box spirals too are unusual, and I would advise purchasing these from a nursery ready-trained. Nathaniel Lloyd, in his *Garden Craftsmanship in Yew and Box* (1925), describes how to make them by twisting the main stem of a young tree around a stake stuck into the ground and, as the plant slowly grows, clipping it into shape, but it does require a sure hand.

The proportions of this garden are exactly right, with a path wide enough to take a wheelbarrow, and the beds narrow enough to be reached easily for the inevitable

Opposite A vista towards gate piers of yew. The main structure is perfectly symmetrical, with yew walls, a central path and four domes of golden box accentuating the central opening. Within this symmetry, herbs add a more casual, exuberant touch.

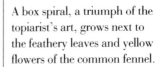

A box spiral, a triumph of the topiarist's art, grows next to the feathery leaves and yellow flowers of the common fennel.

A detail of the central enclosure. The mint, growing in its round terracotta pot, repeats the circular theme of the golden box and the enclosure itself. Mixed herbs fill the border behind.

maintenance tasks. This is not a garden that looks after itself; many herbs are short-lived and need to be constantly replaced with fresh stock. Most shrubby herbs grow easily from cuttings, and, of course, perennials can be propagated by division, a mere afternoon's work in mid-spring. Other herbs are far too prolific, and unwanted seedlings spring up everywhere. With experience, such undesirable seedlings are easily recognized, and hand weeded or hoed.

Within the yew walls there is a pleasant play of symmetry and asymmetry, of formal and informal. The yew, box and paving provide the formal symmetry; the shrubby, perennial, biennial and annual herbs provide the rest. Many herbs are naturally untidy and chaotic, and look best when in a formal setting. There is, though, a world of difference between untidy and chaotic and, here, for example, the floppy cotton lavender and lavender have been allowed to occasionally break the hard boundary between path and planting. A pot of mint is in evidence – if planting it in the garden proper, remember to box its roots for it spreads like wildfire in all directions.

Most herbs have small or even insignificant flowers, but in a well-planned garden, such as this one, I never mind the absence of blazing colour. The greens, greys, yellows and purples of the foliage – the latter colour coming from purple sage – make a lively combination. The tiny, intensely yellow button-like flowers of cotton lavender, the mild pink globe-like flowers of chive and the spikes of lavender and veronica stand out against this soft, multi-coloured background like tiny dabs of paint.

Out-of-season, the garden will look mildly empty but not desperately depressing, saved by its backbone of evergreens. It could be made more interesting by the incorporation of winter- and spring-flowering bulbs. The pale or deep blue netted iris, the bright yellow winter aconite and the sweetly scented lily of the valley, are just a few of the many possibilities.

The way to set about making a herb garden of this sort is much the same as for a formal country-house garden (see pages 64-69). However, the location is more important because herbs need sun and free-draining soil as well as shelter. Whatever the size, such a herb garden would automatically evoke a sense of history. Through the Dark Ages, herb gardening was the only gardening of a vaguely ornamental nature, although the herbs were grown for medicinal purposes. In the present century, herbs have enjoyed a tremendous revival, because of renewed interest in alternative medicine and the culinary arts. No longer an appendage to the vegetable garden, the herb garden is gaining new-found status as garden art.

KEY TO PLAN

1. *Taxus baccata*
2. *Buxus sempervirens*
3. *Melissa officinalis*
4. *Origanum onites*
5. *Peucedanum graveolens*
6. *Artemisia abrotanum*
7. *Petroselinum crispum*
8. *Thymus vulgaris*
9. *Allium schoenoprasum*
10. *Foeniculum vulgare*
11. *Sanguisorba minor*
12. *Anthriscus cerefolium*
13. *Thymus × citriodorus*
14. *Origanum marjorana*
15. *Coriandrum sativum*
16. *Hyssopus officinalis*
17. *Ocimum basilicum*
18. *Laurus nobilis*
19. *Allium sativum*
20. *Santolina chamaecyparissus*
21. *Rumex acetosa*
22. *Salvia officinalis*
23. *Mentha spicata*
24. *Satureja montana*
25. *Artemisia dracunculus*
26. *Asperula odorata*
27. *Borago officinalis*
28. *Angelica archangelica*
29. *Allium giganteum*
30. *Pimpinella anisum*
31. *Rosmarinus officinalis*
32. *Lavandula spica*
33. *Salvia officinalis* 'Purpurascens'

At the entrance to the herb garden is a small outdoor room, paved in stone and furnished with terracotta pots and a tiny water feature. Notice how the herbs, overspilling the beds, offset the formality of the clipped yew and box, and soften the hard edges of the paving.

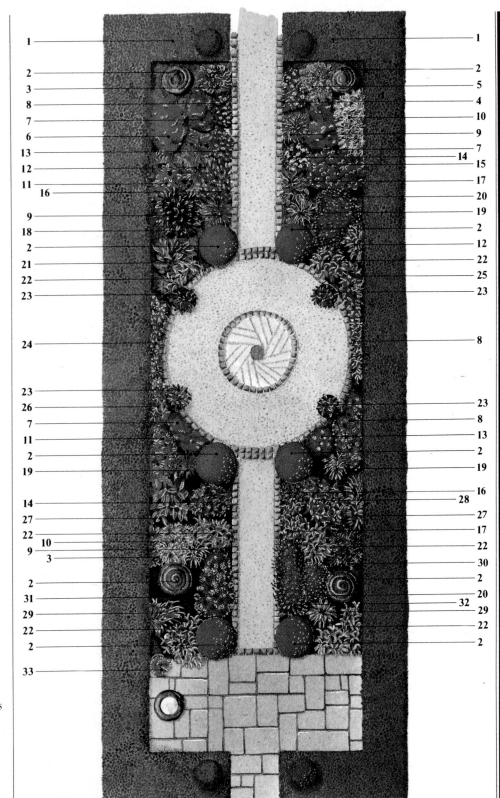

The
INFORMAL
GARDEN

*

This is one of the most successful solutions I have ever seen for coping with that walled patch of earth that lurks behind small nineteenth-century terraced houses. The owner has created a private paradise by the very simple means of combining paving with occasional gaps for plants, building steps and a raised flowerbed, throwing a pergola arch over it all and covering the walls with trellis.

The result is the opposite of that of the usual formal town garden with its use of straight lines, false perspective and statuary, which would have been wholly inappropriate for this modest house. Instead, the lines are softer, while the profusion and planting are more typical of the English cottage garden: foxgloves, lady's mantle, columbines, forget-me-nots, irises, white tulips, ferns and philadelphus. A huge yellow climbing rose forms an arch above, drawing the two sides of the composition together, and the trellis-covered walls are deliberately obscured by ivy and honeysuckle.

Any garden containing rampant self-seeders, as this one does, is bound to change from year to year, virtually of its own accord. Forget-me-not (*Myosotis sylvatica*) and foxglove (*Digitalis* spp) are two biennials that become self-perpetuating, once introduced. A scattering of forget-me-not seed produces plants in most unpredictable places; they have not been included in the planting plan for this reason. The columbine (*Aquilegia* spp) and lady's mantle (*Alchemilla mollis*) are equally prolific.

Everything here has to be carefully nurtured and arranged, the potted plants must be taken indoors when it gets cold, the paving kept free of weeds and the self-seeders kept under surveillance, for the charming informal effect is highly calculated. What could have been a dull backyard has been manipulated brilliantly to form a dishevelled, all-year picture for those looking out from behind the large plate glass window.

The garden in early summer, with lady's mantle, forget-me-nots, lilies, foxgloves, roses and tulips in bloom.

KEY TO PLAN

1. *Pittosporum tenuifolium* 'Warnham Gold'
2. *Ceanothus* 'Gloire de Versailles'
3. *Hedera helix* var.
4. *Clematis viticella* 'Alba Luxurians'
5. *Magnolia × loebneri* 'Merrill'
6. *Lonicera periclymenum*
7. *Buddleia × weyerana* 'Golden Glory'
8. *Camellia × williamsii* 'Cornish Snow'
9. *Matthiola incana*
10. *Jasminum nudiflorum*
11. *Iris* Pacific Coast hybrid
12. *Jasminum officinale*
13. *Rhododendron* 'Coral'
14. *Alchemilla mollis*
15. *Digitalis purpurea*
16. *Buddleia fallowiana* 'Alba'
17. *Rosa* 'New Dawn'
18. *Dryopteris filix-mas*
19. *Miscanthus sinensis* 'Variegatus'
20. *Euphorbia palustris*
21. *Hebe* hybrid
22. *Clematis macropetala*
23. *Epimedium* hybrid
24. *Petunia × hybrida* var.
25. *Tulipa* hybrid
26. *Rosa* 'Golden Shower'
27. *Philadelphus* 'Bouquet Blanc'
28. *Acer japonicum* 'Aureum'
29. *Hedera helix* 'Goldheart'
30. *Nandina domestica*
31. *Helleborus foetidus*
32. *Lamium maculatum*
33. *Rhododendron trichostomum*
34. *Solanum jasminoides* 'Album'
35. *Forsythia × intermedia*
36. *Rosa* 'Lawrence Johnson'
37. *Clematis orientalis* 'Bill Mackenzie'
38. *Camellia japonica* 'Magnoliaeflora'
39. *Anemone japonica* 'Alba'
40. *Aquilegia × hybrida*
41. *Iris foetidissima*
42. *Magnolia × loebneri* 'Leonard Messel'
43. *Clematis* 'Huldine'
44. *Euonymus fortunei radicans*
45. *Elaeagnus pungens*
46. *Convallaria majalis*
47. *Houttuynia cordata*
48. *Rosa* 'Vespa'
49. *Rhododendron fragrantissima*
50. *Hosta* hybrid
51. *Hydrangea macrophylla* 'Blue Nile'
52. *Lonicera × purpusii*
53. *Hedera colchica* 'Dentata'
54. *Hydrangea arborescens* 'Grandiflora'

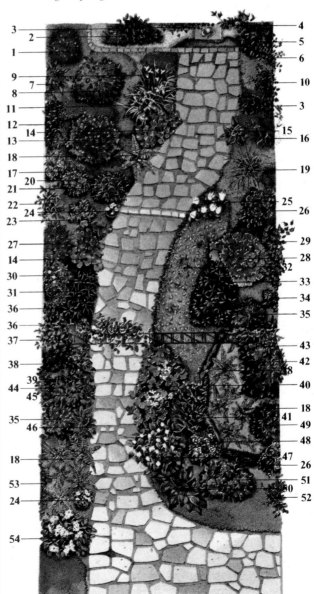

The
COUNTRY-HOUSE
GARDEN

*

In my imagination, I can at once people this garden with elegant Edwardian women carrying lace parasols and young men in attendance wearing striped blazers and straw boaters. Although the area is small and the layout utterly simple, this garden evokes all the glories of the English country-house garden before 1914. The formally clipped yew and box are living architecture, a classic foil to the cascading roses. These hedges provide a simple, sombre background against which the silver-leaved plants and herbaceous perennials can display their summer glory. In winter, the yew and box remain, their substantial presence making up for the fickleness of herbaceous perennials and the sad state of roses then. And, as well as delighting the eye, the garden has been designed for fragrance – the heady scent of roses and dianthus mingling with the more astringent aroma of cotton lavender and the old-fashioned perfume of lavender.

The success of this design depends entirely on its geometry and the maintenance of that geometry. If hedge-clipping and pruning were to cease, out of laziness, lack of time, or 'kindness' to the plants, all would be lost. Unpruned roses quickly become unruly, unproductive members of the garden community. The yew and box are long-term residents (and will probably outlive all of us) but grey- and silver-leaved plants are relatively short-lived. They needn't be included, of course, but if they are, they will need replacing every five or six years, which I think is a small price to pay for their elegant presence. The perennials will need autumn maintenance, but there are relatively few of them and, because the beds are small, they are easily reached from the paths.

The strong, flat, geometric design of this garden is emphasized by the brick paths and clipped hedges. Informal planting within this framework adds a pleasant contrast, and distant trees add a change of scale and height.

Below A formal garden structure containing exuberant, more relaxed planting. In the background, beyond the yew hedge, is a cane framework, to which young pleached limes are trained.

High summer in a yellow, green and white garden. High-level yellows are provided by climbing roses. Closer to the ground, helianthemums, hostas, shrub roses and lady's mantle continue the theme.

The plan of this garden is square, the boundary marked by a young yew hedge. Narrow paths of brick laid in the traditional basketweave pattern repeat the square theme within the yew boundary. A cruciform network of inner paths is laid at a 45° angle to the outer brick square, and divides it into a series of rectangular and triangular beds around a central, diamond-shaped bed. It is a formal garden plan on which endless variations are possible. A piece of graph paper with the scale of your garden worked out, a sharp pencil and your own imagination are the prerequisites.

Instead of brick, stone could be used. If you choose the reconstituted variety, the euphemistic name for concrete, instead of natural stone, do avoid those viciously red, green and yellow ochre ones, and stick to grey. York stone paving is lovely, but expensive and slippery in wet weather. Gravel is a possibility, but it needs a black plastic underlay to prevent weeds coming through, and edging strips to keep the gravel in its rightful, proper place. Victorian rope-edged tiles are pretty, although difficult to find. Real gluttons for punishment might choose grass paths, which are beautiful if meticulously weeded, mowed and trimmed, but disastrous if they are not.

The colour control in this garden is total: predominantly green, green-grey, yellow and white. White with pink or blue could look as extraordinary, and so could all white, but the balance must be perfect. What happens in the middle of the garden is very important since all the geometry leads the eye to that point. Here, Arabella Lennox-Boyd, the designer, has filled the central bed with the pure white rose 'Moonlight'. If the roses had been yellow, the effect, I think, would immediately have been spoilt. Other suitable centrepieces would be a sundial, statue or an Italianate wellhead. Anything too tall would give away the secret of the garden's small size.

Yellow roses fill the four rectangular beds surrounding the centre and provide blocks of repeating colour. The theme is repeated in the four corners of each rectangular bed; tiny controlled displays of contrasting colour made up of purple-leaved sage, blue-leaved rue, yellow-leaved hostas and even blue-flowering agapanthus. All are given the same backing of yellow roses and the same hedging of mixed yellow helianthemums.

The triangular outer beds have been kept very simple. The four truncated triangles in the corners contain green santolina edged in box, which is clipped just higher than the hedge and is simply a plane of colour; those in between are edged in grey santolina and filled with foaming yellow lady's mantle.

Between the central formal garden and the yew hedge

A small triangular bed edged with cotton lavender (*Santolina chamaecyparissus*) and infilled with lady's mantle (*Alchemilla mollis*). The former is easily propagated from cuttings; the latter self-seeds freely.

is a border punctuated with pergolas bearing climbing yellow roses. A brick tongue extends from the square to form a pergola-backed seating area. From its central position, the beauty of the geometry can be admired in a leisurely way. Note how subtle the grey wooden seat is compared to a white one. Left unpainted, its own natural colour has faded to almost no colour at all.

There are no trees within the central square but large distant trees provide a backdrop. If your garden is not well endowed with background trees, consider incorporating a dwarf apple tree in each corner.

This is a garden not only to walk in but to look down on – the pattern of the geometry becomes clearer when seen from above, from first-floor windows or a raised terrace. Alternatively, the ground can be treated as a raised viewing platform by sinking the garden. The soil must be free draining, or the sunken formal garden may become waterlogged whenever it rains, something that roses and grey-leaved plants simply cannot bear.

This is definitely an early summer garden, which raises the question of what happens the rest of the year. In the days when large gardens were more prevalent than they are now, a garden often contained a series of garden 'rooms', such as this one. Each 'room' was planted according to a different theme, such as the all-white garden or all-grey garden. If a formal garden is your only garden 'room', it must be attractive, or at least not unattractive, most of the year. The evergreen and evergrey hedging helps. And so would planting snowdrops, *en masse*, under the roses; the greeny-grey snowdrop foliage dies down well before the early summer show, and there is no nasty overlap of dying foliage among the fresh new growth. I would use yellow or white bedding tulips as blocks of spring colour, planting the bulbs in autumn and digging them up as soon as flowering is over.

KEY TO PLAN

1. *Buxus sempervirens*
2. *Santolina neapolitana*
3. *Santolina chamaecyparissus*
4. *Genista aetnensis*
5. *Ceanothus arboreus* 'Trewithen Blue'
6. *Delphinium elatum* 'Tiddles'
7. *Syringa vulgaris* 'Mme Lemoine'
8. *Rosa* 'Little White Pet'
9. *Alopecurus pratensis* 'Aureus'
10. *Rosa* 'Yvonne Rabier'
11. *Rosa* 'Canary Bird'
12. *Paeonia mlokosewitschii*
13. *Alchemilla mollis*
14. *Hosta sieboldiana* 'Elegans'
15. *Taxus baccata* 'Aurea'
16. *Artemisia abrotanum*
17. *Lavandula spica* 'Hidcote'
18. *Rosa* 'Alister Stella Grey'
19. *Helleborus lividus corsicus*
20. *Lavandula spica* 'Alba'
21. *Hosta fortunei* 'Albopicta'
22. *Anthemis cupaniana*
23. *Helianthemum nummularium* Mixed vars: 'Ben Dearg', 'Coppernob', 'Snowball', 'The Bride', 'Wisley Primrose'
24. *Agapanthus* 'Headbourne Hybrids'
25. *Rosa* 'Norwich Union' (syn 'Peter Beales')
26. *Ruta graveolens* 'Jackman's Blue'
27. *Hosta fortunei* 'Aureomarginata'
28. *Ballota pseudo-dictamnus*
29. *Perovskia atriplicifolia* 'Blue Spire'
30. *Robinia pseudoacacia* 'Frisia'
31. *Convolvulus cneorum*
32. *Rhus cotinus* 'Notcutts Variety'
33. *Prunus* 'Tai Haku'
34. *Lupinus arboreus* 'Golden Spire'
35. *Iris* 'Jane Phillips'
36. *Syringa vulgaris* 'Lamartine'
37. *Paeonia lactiflora* 'White Wings'
38. *Phlomis samia*
39. *Centranthus ruber* 'Albus'
40. *Salvia officinalis* 'Tricolor'
41. *Dianthus* 'Mrs Sinkins'
42. *Rosa* 'Moonlight'
43. *Salvia officinalis* 'Purpurascens'
44. *Hosta* 'Thomas Hogg'
45. *Carpinus betulus* 'Fastigiata'
46. *Yucca filamentosa* 'Variegata'
47. *Rosa rugosa* 'Alba'
48. *Dorycnium suffruticosum*
49. *Taxus baccata*

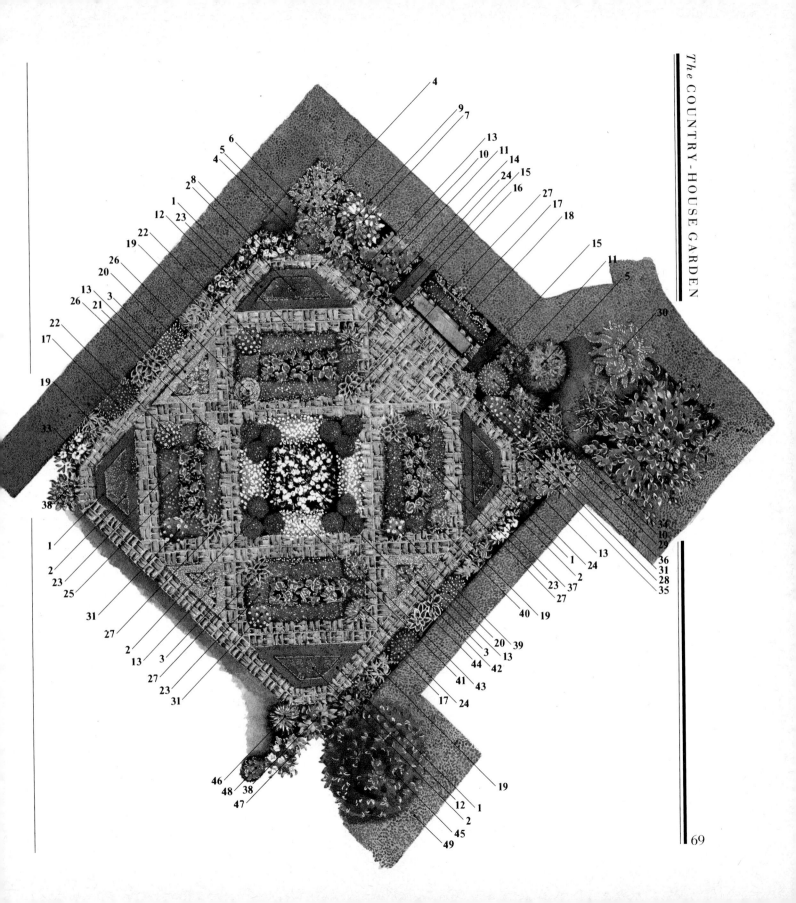

The
ARCHITECTURAL
GARDEN

*

There is a healthy, no-nonsense modernist approach to this garden. It is totally devoid of nostalgia and classical romanticism – two major ingredients of most garden visions – and is nonetheless wholly successful for that. We find ourselves firmly in the present in an area designed for ease of maintenance and *alfresco* living in a sunny climate. The gardener who follows the romantic tradition confuses boundaries; here they are firmly stated by garden walls and the house itself, with its arcaded entrance. The result is an open-air room, typical of the Mediterranean or West Coast of America. If it is too hot, the luncheon table is moved from open terrace to the adjacent loggia; if it is pleasantly warm, it is as easily moved out into the garden area.

This is as little demanding of labour as it is reasonable to expect in a garden with so luxuriant planting. It is virtually all building and its planting is of the simplest kind. It will be time, not work, that will enrich and mellow it still further. Even the beds are raised so that it is not necessary to bend down to tend or prune a flower or bush. And yet, for all its practicality, it certainly retains a style – generated by the architecture of the house – of which the garden is an integral part. In fact, this is not a garden to copy, but rather a model which architects and owners can adapt. Everything here is very sensitively proportioned. You only have to study the careful placing of the pond and the beds and above all, the phasing of the widths of the pond, its retaining wall and the path running through the garden to realise that. The flight of steps and the pierced wall, again, are perfectly positioned with openings giving tantalizing glimpses of the country-side. Not only does such a wall give protection and privacy, but it dramatizes the contrast between the contained space of the garden and the open space beyond.

The planting is elementary and uncomplicated, drawing both on indigenous and exotic material. There are few trees but each is sharply contrasted in form, foliage and colour: the fast-growing *Eucalyptus gunnii* with its distinctive oval grey leaves, the spiky-leaved Italian stone pine (*Pinus pinea*), another fast-grower, mimosa (*Acacia*

Left Alfresco lunch by a raised pool in the garden of a holiday home. Minimum maintenance was a top priority in the garden design.

Above A *tableau* of clay pipes, stones, pebbles and water in the Oriental manner. Cotoneaster and Japanese maple mingle with the *objets trouvés*.

dealbata), with feathery foliage coated with silvery down, and the curiously twisted corkscrew willow (*Salix matsudana* 'Tortuosa') adds valuable winter interest. The shrubs and perennials selected – lavender, iris, acanthus, cotoneaster and St John's wort among them – are tough and uncomplaining, requiring little attention apart from an annual trim. In this respect, they are ideal ingredients for a holiday home garden.

Unfortunately, the choice of colour is not always happy here, with hot yellows and reds together – not all architects are as sensitive with colour as they are with form. How much pleasanter this garden would be if the violent red floribunda roses had been creamy yellow, and the red pelargoniums had not been surrounded by harsh yellow blossom.

Although there can be a tendency in architectural gardens to pave over too much in an attempt to keep the natural world at bay, the firm paths and boxed beds do cut weeding to a minimum and provide the equivalent of root pruning. The architectural garden is a play of hard and soft. In short, the valid structural contribution of the architect needs to be complemented by a painterly eye.

71

A view beyond the raised pool
to the house, with the planting
just beginning to soften the
firm architectural framework.
Carefully selected and
arranged groups of large
pebbles and stones create a
contemporary still life.

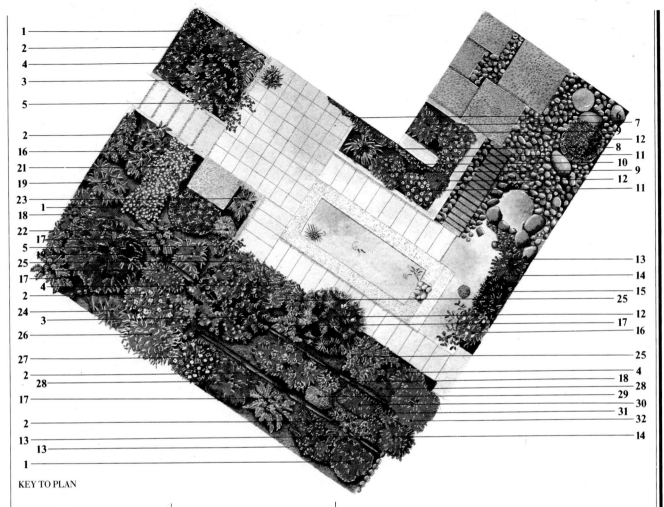

KEY TO PLAN

1. *Rosmarinus officinalis*
2. *Rosa* hybrid
3. *Eucalyptus gunnii*
4. *Lavandula spica*
5. *Hedera helix*
6. *Clematis montana*
7. *Fuchsia* hybrid
8. *Crinum moorei*
9. *Linaria alpina*
10. *Cotoneaster wardii*
11. *Limnanthes douglasii*
12. *Pinus pinea*
13. *Cotoneaster dammeri*
14. *Rhododendron rubiginosum*
15. *Acer palmatum* 'Atropurpureum'
16. *Cotoneaster* 'Cornubia'
17. *Acanthus mollis*
18. *Euphorbia polychroma (E. epithymoides)*
19. *Fatsia japonica*
20. *Acacia dealbata*
21. *Kolkwitzia amabilis*
22. *Artemisia* sp.
23. *Nicotiana affinis (N. alata)*
24. *Iris* hybrid
25. *Hypericum polyphyllum (H. olympicum)*
26. *Salix matsudana* 'Tortuosa'
27. *Myrtus communis*
28. *Cytisus canariensis*
29. *Hippophaë rhamnoides*
30. *Erica arborea*
31. *Hypericum calycinum*
32. *Nandina domestica*

The
COTTAGE
GARDEN

*

The very mention of a cottage garden evokes an instant image of a picturesque Victorian age – a profusion of romantic, old-fashioned and sweet-smelling flowers, primroses, violets, foxgloves and lavender intermingled with herbs such as rosemary and rue. At its best, as in the example here, the cottage garden embodies everything to prompt nostalgia for a simple lost way of life that probably never was. Of course, there is nothing wrong with that, for every garden creates a dream world.

For those who undertake such a venture I would advise caution. The cottage garden is for the enthusiast since it needs constant attention all the year round. In addition, it is not, I believe, a style that can be lifted and put down easily in the city. It requires a backdrop of building rather than architecture, and prefers a rural setting. Few seemingly so artless forms of garden design can so quickly slip over into pure kitsch.

It is precisely the fact that there is no formal structure which makes this type of garden peculiarly difficult, and a challenge to manage successfully. There is almost always a straight path of stone, gravel or other good natural material (not synthetic slabs) to the front door with, on either side, an asymmetrical planting in clumps arranged according to height. The walls marking the boundaries and enclosing such a garden should be stone or a hedge of yew, holly, quickthorn or beech, or a tapestry hedge intermingling all four. Arbours and pergolas of larch (trellis at a pinch) form the only plant-bearing structure and all forms of garden ornament are out of place as they strike a note of gentrification. Indeed, you can sum up a cottage garden by a list of what it should not include. That means all varieties of dwarf conifer and rhododendron and virulently coloured modern shrub roses. There should also be no manicured lawn and no artificial pond, only an area of rough-cut grass with fruit trees (dwarf rooting stock). As a bonus, the rough grass provides the ideal excuse for planting drifts of species narcissus, and their leaves have time to die down before the first, early summer mow.

The essence of the planting is a calculated lack of

Left The key to this cottage garden is informal profusion, asymmetry and harmony of colour. The house is seen through drifts and clumps of old-fashioned flowers, arranged by height and colour.

Above A slightly dishevelled, but still pleasing, congregation of plants: white delphiniums, lilies, lamb's tongue and a hedgerow incursion, cow parsley.

Below The garden at its apogee, as if awaiting the brush of Renoir or Fantin Latour. The plants are planted in bold clumps, but given enough freedom to mingle with their neighbours.

Right A close up of a small section of the flower-packed garden. Columbines, sweet Williams, lupins, delphiniums and an 'uninvited' carpet of scarlet pimpernel form an explosion of colour.

obvious plan, arranging perennials, biennials, annuals and herbs in groups around shrubs. Drifts of plants fill the garden; here, in early summer, Canterbury bells, sweet Williams and lavender are set off by the stinging yellow of yarrow. Lupins, delphiniums and mullein add height, with the mullein providing the coolest silver-grey relief to the hot palette surrounding it. There are no large shrubs in the garden illustrated, although lilacs and philadelphus, or mock orange, fit comfortably in cottage gardens, and both have lovely early summer flowers and scent.

A cottage garden would be unworthy of the name if it lacked roses. The old garden roses that were popular before the development of Hybrid Tea roses, in the late nineteenth century, are now making a comeback. Many gardeners have had their fill of Hybrid Teas and Floribundas, and are choosing instead earlier roses. Briar roses, cabbage roses, Gallicas, China roses, damask roses, hybrid perpetuals and moss roses can be had from specialist rose nurseries and, on a smaller sale, from more enlightened garden centres. Grow jasmine, clematis or honeysuckle intermingled with climbing roses for a doubly overgrown effect.

The number of suitable perennials, biennials and annuals is enormous. The perennials include: columbine, mullein, gypsophila, peony, lupin, delphinium, phlox, Solomon's seal, day lily, lady's mantle, yarrow and lamb's tongue, or lamb's ear. Add to these the annuals and biennials: sunflower, larkspur, foxglove, stock, tobacco plant, snapdragon, cornflower, marigold (calendulas, not the ghastly *Tagetes erecta*), wallflower, sweet William, forget-me-not, Canterbury bell, hollyhock, candytuft and nasturtium.

Lavender features heavily in this garden, while southernwood (*Artemisia abrotanum*) makes a more subtle appearance. Traditional herbs worthy of inclusion are rosemary, rue, borage, catmint, chamomile, cotton lavender, dill, lemon balm, angelica and sage. Creeping thyme, saxifrage and thrift can be tucked into the crevices of stonework. For winter colour, rely on snowdrops, crocuses and the netted iris (*Iris reticulata*) and follow on with cottage garden tulips in spring.

The result of such a garden is pure enchantment. It is the dream picture on the packet of seeds given to children – 'Cottage Garden Mix', come to fruition. But those who essay it have to be a combination of Gertrude Jekyll and Claude Monet. Their reward, as their labour, will be never ending.

The
GRAVEL
GARDEN

*

This long narrow garden shows how surprisingly attractive shrubs look against gravel. A simple essay almost entirely in evergreens and 'evergreys', this is a marvellous, casual-looking garden with an asymmetrical arrangement of rounded, clipped or pruned shrubby plants: box, santolina and sage interspersed with dwarf pittosporum, lavender, senecio and rosemary.

I like the crunch of gravel underfoot and it is easy to maintain, requiring only raking and rolling from time to time, and the occasional judicious use of weedkiller to keep it looking immaculate. The ground must first be laid out and levelled, then covered with a layer of small stones, for adequate drainage, followed by a finishing layer of gravel.

The introduction of large terracotta pots is worthy of serious consideration. Careful positioning will give 'architecture' and punctuation to even the most informal of plantings. In Mediterranean countries the use of such pots is part of the gardening norm – almost every gardener makes use of them, often placing them on top of plinths for added emphasis. They embody a means of instant garden design virtually lost in northern countries, but it is well worth considering. The pots need to be large enough to have any impact which can cause problems if you don't have the space to overwinter them indoors – frost can be extremely damaging in colder areas. There is, however, no reason why this style should not become more widely copied and adapted to climes which have some assured stretch of reasonable weather.

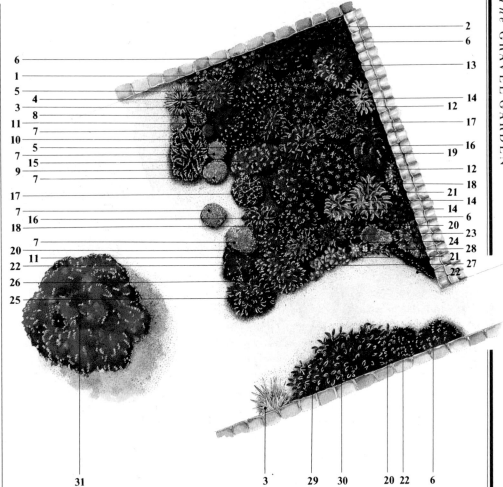

LEFT A view of the asymmetrical gravel garden with, to the left, two *Robinia pseudoacacia* underplanted with *Choisya ternata*. The central planting is a composition of rounded clipped and pruned evergreen and 'everygrey' plants.

KEY TO PLAN

1. *Rosa* hybrid
2. *Lonicera japonica*
3. *Yucca gloriosa*
4. *Pittosporum tobira* 'Variegatum'
5. *Buxus sempervirens*
6. *Iberis sempervirens*
7. *Santolina chamaecyparissus*
8. *Acantholimon venustum*
9. *Juniperus* var.
10. *Dianthus* var.
11. *Salvia officinalis*
12. *Rosmarinus officinalis*
13. *Myrtus communis*
14. *Stachys lanata*
15. *Potentilla mandshurica*
16. *Centaurea montana*
17. *Lavandula spica*
18. *Pittosporum tobira*
19. *Berberis × stenophylla*
20. *Cotoneaster wardii*
21. *Anaphalis triplinervis*
22. *Senecio elegans*
23. *Helichrysum plicatum*
24. *Santolina neapolitana*
25. *Euonymus microphylla*
26. *Senecio laxifolius*
27. *Alchemilla mollis*
28. *Artemisia arborescens*
29. *Centaurea dealbata*
30. *Carpenteria californica*
31. *Robinia pseudoacacia*

The
MULTI-LEVEL
GARDEN

*

This is a classic town garden, a vision of abundance in a minute area. It has been designed to take full advantage of a sloping site, and the formula could easily be adapted for a house with a basement looking out on to a well and access to the garden via the first-floor level. The slope also means that the garden is seen straight on from at least two floors of the house.

The structure here is very simple: a tiny terrace immediately outside the garden door leads up a flight of steps to a second small paved area. In a small urban garden such as this, lawn is nearly always out of place. The space normally occupied by a pocket-handkerchief lawn is filled instead with cleverly sited focal points: a statue of a Baccante, surrounded by seasonal planting and framed by the lacy fronds of *Artemisia arborescens*; an island herbaceous border backing on to an ornamental pool and fountain, and a decorative arch. Moreover, the garden cannot be observed in its entirety from any one viewpoint, and its boundaries are obscured. I think that the decision to paint the back of the house white offsets the foliage and blossom, and contributes greatly to the extraordinary feeling of utter freshness.

Plants are selected for their durability as well as for their beauty. The richly scented, pinky-white greenhouse jasmine (*Jasminum polyanthum*) flourishes in the shelter and warmth of a city garden. In mild winters, tender fuchsias are left out with impunity. Tender, ivy-leaved geraniums could be treated likewise, and grow big enough to cover a tall arch with pale pink blossom.

There are seasonal shows of colour against a backdrop of permanent green: Mexican orange blossom, cypress, box, masses of ivies, bergenias, evergreen helle-bores. The floral palette is limited to white, pale yellow, blue, mauve and the complete range of pinks. Each bed has a predominant colour theme, merging slightly with the adjacent colours. In spring, there is a profusion of wallflowers, forget-me-nots and tulips. In summer, the traditional herbaceous border comes into its own, at the same time as the climbing and shrub roses. Every available space is packed with bedding plants – begonias,

tobacco plants, petunias, busy Lizzies – and the trellis-topped walls are clothed with climbers.

This is a garden lover's garden. It exudes great care and attention in the maintenance of all the potted plants, the emptying of the fountain in winter, the pruning of the wisteria and roses, the annual bedding out of more delicate flowers, such as the forest of busy Lizzie and the tuberous-rooted begonias. Even the charming bouquet of pink double tulips and blue hyacinths around the foot of the statue represent planning during the previous autumn. Nothing has been left to chance, and the result is pure delight.

Immediately outside the
house is a small sitting area.
Originally paved in concrete
and sporting three manhole
covers, attractive stone paving
was laid over the entire area
and set in dry sand, to allow
access to the manhole covers.
The wisteria, honeysuckle,
clematis and roses swathing
the walls provide scent and
colour seen from indoors and
out; baby's tears carpets the
tiny beds with green.

The first floor balcony overlooks a vista of delights. A profusion of mixed planting achieves virtually total enclosure and privacy.

KEY TO PLAN

1. *Lonicera japonica*
2. *Ceanothus* 'Gloire de Versailles'
3. *Lonicera pileata*
4. *Osmanthus delavayi*
5. *Wisteria sinensis*
6. *Hebe brachysiphon*
7. *Stachys lanata*
8. *Iberis sempervirens*
9. *Cupressus* var.
10. *Euonymus fortunei* var.
11. *Pittosporum tobira*
12. *Lavandula spica*
13. *Pachysandra terminalis*
14. *Viburnum* sp.
15. *Jasminum polyanthum*
16. *Choisya ternata*
17. *Nicotiana alata*
18. *Hosta undulata*
19. *Artemisia arborescens*
20. *Sarcococca humilis*
21. *Aquilegia vulgaris*
22. *Crinum moorei*
23. *Hosta fortunei*
24. *Polygonum campanulatum*
25. *Potentilla fruticosa*
26. Bedding annuals
27. *Lamium galeobdolon*
28. *Bergenia cordifolia* 'Purpurea'
29. *Philadelphus* 'Virginal'
30. *Vitis coignetiae*
31. *Hypericum calycinum*
32. *Hedera helix* var.
33. *Santolina chamaecyparissus*
34. *Artemisia ludoviciana*
35. *Petunia* × *hybrida*
36. *Helleborus foetidus*
37. *Dryopteris filix-mas*
38. *Rosa* hybrids
39. *Senecio laxifolius*
40. *Ruta graveolens*
41. *Rosmarinus officinalis*
42. *Lunaria annua*
43. *Cotoneaster salicifolius*
44. *Pulmonaria picta*
45. *Jasminum nudiflorum*
46. *Clematis* hybrid
47. *Liriope muscari*
48. *Ceratostigma willmottianum*
49. *Iris foetidissima*
50. *Buxus sempervirens*
51. *Bergenia cordifolia*
52. *Acanthus mollis*
53. *Fuchsia* hybrids
54. *Tellima grandiflora*
55. *Bergenia crassifolia*
56. *Impatiens wallerana*

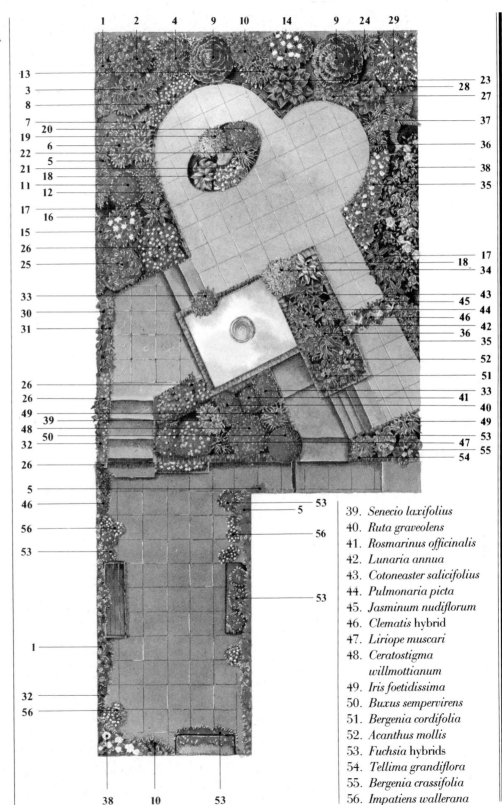

The
ROMANTIC GARDEN

*

Here is a country garden which is so heady with romance that the only element missing is the lady of the Camellias in a huge beribboned straw hat and a billowing crinoline of sprigged muslin. In this garden we seem to step back a century to the golden era of the rose, the one flower which epitomizes the romantic age. The spectacular effect has been achieved by a lavish use of rambler and climbing roses. These roses hang in great swags scenting a garden seat, scramble over a wooden bridge transforming it into an enchanted walkway, tumble down a bank to be reflected in the water of the canal below and frame the house so that only the windows peep through.

This garden is only 15 years old but already it looks a survivor of an earlier more leisured age. It is essentially a simple garden, consisting of a narrow rectangular area between the canal and the walls of the house. This is traversed by a stone path ending in the rose pavilion. The closeness of the water pervades the atmosphere, with its own romantic connotations and its reflective qualities. So, too, does the quality of the architectural backdrop. One has the feeling that it would be hard to go wrong, horticulturally, with such a stage setting.

A row of perfectly conical conifers is planted at regular intervals along the length of the garden. These are a form of dwarf spruce (*Picea glauca albertiana* 'Conica'), originally found in the Canadian Rockies, which grow naturally into a conical shape. Yew or box could be substituted, but both need careful training and clipping to achieve a similar shape.

Between the formal conifers and the water's edge there is a tangled planting of herbaceous plants, vying with each other for space and half tumbling over the wall. Chief among these is the sun-loving red valerian (*Centranthus ruber*) and its white flowered form, *C.r.* 'Albus'. There are the biennials, mullein (*Verbascum bombyciferum*) and foxglove (*Digitalis purpurea*) with yellow and palest pink flower spikes respectively. Herbaceous plants are used as infill between the conifers and path: white geraniums, blue campanulas and ornamental onions add summer colour, as do the apple-blossom pink

The view from the canal shows the rose-covered bridge and one corner of the tiny narrow garden which stretches to the water's edge. The water lilies reduce the reflective quality of the water's surface, but provide flowers in season and a verdant, painterly texture. Mature trees complete the leafy setting.

flowers of the escallonia.

There is clematis to provide early colour, but it is the rose which is the real star of this garden. Each one has been chosen for its vigour and traditional appearance. Even 'Constance Spry', a modern shrub rose dating only from 1960, has the appearance and fragrance of nineteenth-century Provence, or cabbage, roses; its arching growth habit makes it an ideal bower over the stone seat. Two climbers meet over the entrance. The fragrant Bourbon climber, 'Zephirine Drouhin', displays its cerise-pink flowers once in summer, and again in autumn, making it a very valuable rose indeed: the other rose, 'Pink Cloud', is also modern (dating from 1952), fragrant and repeat-flowering. Two wonderful rambling roses tumble over the bridge: 'François Juranville' has long, flexible stems, ideal for training along the railings, and deeply scented, rich pink flowers, while 'Veilchenblau' is distinguished by its purplish-violet blooms that are tinged blue at maturity.

This garden celebrates the beauty of the rose. Each section is devoted to a special category of rose: the albas, the centifolias, the moss roses, the gallicas, the damask roses and so on, says its creator... 'We have bought plants in France, England, Switzerland and Denmark.' This degree of commitment is not essential but you would need a fully illustrated dictionary of roses and a good rose supplier who stocks a large repertory, especially of the old varieties. Visiting gardens open to the public also fires the imagination. After this research, begin by establishing the palette. Avoid the hectic electrifying colours of recent cultivars, fierce oranges, yellows and reds, and build up a colour sequence that avoids sharp contrasts. Remember a little red goes a very long way and a red rose against a red brick wall looks really awful. Stick instead to soft whites, creams, pinks and yellows. Any painting of a vase of roses by Fantin Latour will help you.

An interest in roses can easily become an obsession, as few other flowers are so rich in history or romantic association. Reading rose catalogues is a beguiling experience, with their mesmerizing vocabularies and poetic names such as 'Souvenir de Malmaison', 'Maiden's

The *pièce de résistance*: an old wooden bridge, complete with finials, treated as a pergola. Rambling roses from both banks are trained along the railings, in some places entirely hiding their supports. One is the pink-flowered, deeply scented 'François Juranville'; the other is the purplish violet 'Veilchenblau'. Fallen petals show up like glints of light against the dark water, and water lilies in flower repeat the pink theme.

Above An enchanting arbour formed by training the vigorous 'Constance Spry' rose over a simple frame. The arbour makes a charming feature, terminating a path. It offers privacy and fragrance as well as deep shade.

'Fritz Nobis' is a modern
shrub rose – a hybrid of a
species and an old rose. With
its arching sprays of clove-
scented blossoms it is a useful
rose for the back of a border
or for hedging.

Blush', 'Old Blush' and 'Chapeau de Napoleon'. And
there are few other types of garden that come to fruition
as rapidly as rose gardens, since roses are comparatively
simple to cultivate. Climbing and rambling roses need
architecture against which to perform. While few have a
setting for roses as splendid as the one illustrated here,
even an indifferent house can be transformed by roses
trained up the walls. In the garden, such roses can be
trained along fences, over summer houses, up pillars, over
pergolas or even over old fruit trees. My favourites include
the creamy white 'Felicité et Perpetué' (1827); the
marvellous yellow 'Mermaid' (1917), an almost evergreen climber that flowers throughout the summer, even
on a north wall; the legendary pink and gold 'Albertine'
(1921); and the truly amazing *Rosa filipes* 'Kiftsgate'
(1954), with its clusters of creamy-white flowers. The last
is so vigorous that it will engulf a complete house in
flower, given the opportunity.

A formal row of conical spruce visually links the house and garden. Against this formal setting, shrubs and herbaceous plants run riot, jostling each other for space.

The same row of conifers seen from the rear. The clipped box, standard rose and Irish yew in the distance continue the theme of formality. Escallonia and assorted herbaceous perennials fill every available niche and corner with greenery and flowers, and even the joints between the paving stones have been colonized by small ground-hugging plants.

The
JAPANESE
GARDEN

*

This garden is inspired by the purest of Japanese garden traditions, one in which all superfluities and almost all plants have been eliminated – the temple gardens of Zen Buddhism. It appears to have been based on the famous rock garden of Ryuanji Temple at Kyoto, a rectangular plot about the size of a tennis court in which fifteen rocks, divided into five groups, rise out of white sand. Everything the eye encounters, the positioning and relationship between the components, is charged with significance. Sand symbolizes water, and an infinite variety of markings from a rake simulate its flow. The stones are interpreted according to their size, shape, colour and texture. The garden is to be contemplated, not trodden.

Within a modernist context, this formula can be remarkably successful. An enclosed courtyard is important, to create serenity and keep the garden separate from more mundane, perhaps noisier, views and activities. Moss as a ground cover is beautiful and in keeping with the Japanese style. Grass could be substituted, though it lacks the mounded quality of moss, and mowing is a problem. The sand depends for its effect on immaculate presentation; regular raking is essential.

The planting in this garden is sparse and thoughtfully chosen. Evergreen cotoneaster is trained against a stone wall, and an ornamental vine (*Vitis coignetiae*) clambers up and along the loggia. Two free-standing shrubs, *Rhododendron* Mollis hybrid, with its rich autumn leaf tints, and a Japanese maple (*Acer palmatum*) frame the view and complete the scene. No one in the West can hope to do more than borrow elements of this tradition of garden style, in which a symbolic landscape in miniature is meant to evoke one's deepest feelings about nature.

At the turn of the century, there was a vogue in Europe for *japanoiserie*, and gardens were full of stone lanterns, wooden bridges, tea pavilions, cherry trees and azaleas. In fact, although the Japanese are fond of certain flowers – cherry blossom, azaleas, chrysanthemums and wisteria among them – they are not part of the classical Japanese garden, in which permanence is more important than ephemeral beauty.

90

Left A Western evocation of the temple gardens of Zen Buddhism, with an arrangement of rocks as 'mountains' in a 'sea' of sand raked to simulate the flow of water. Such a garden demands a response from the owner or viewer to the beauty of abstract shape.

Right Across the 'sea' of sand is a loggia from which the garden can be admired and enjoyed. The rocks were chosen for their unusual shapes and placed with great visual sensitivity.

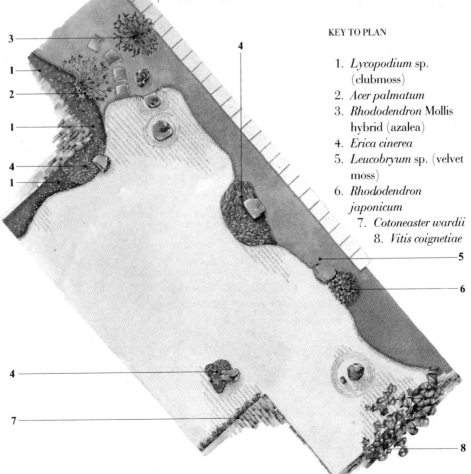

KEY TO PLAN

1. *Lycopodium* sp. (clubmoss)
2. *Acer palmatum*
3. *Rhododendron* Mollis hybrid (azalea)
4. *Erica cinerea*
5. *Leucobryum* sp. (velvet moss)
6. *Rhododendron japonicum*
7. *Cotoneaster wardii*
8. *Vitis coignetiae*

The
DELL
GARDEN

*

Here is a garden that reflects the deeply held beliefs of its designer about the role gardens should play in a period of acute ecological consciousness. His aim is to create, in even the smallest space, an environment which is as 'natural' as possible. The balance in horticultural design terms is, therefore, almost the reverse of the norm. In most gardens the owner's will is imposed on to nature, which is ordered and arranged for his or her convenience. In this garden, human beings come second and are tolerated as observers of a natural process which they are invited to study and admire. The plants are not treated as decoration but as though the garden were an idealized version of their own natural habitat.

The result is like lifting the most beautiful minute dell and depositing it in an ordinary back garden. Its concessions to the normal garden repertory are few and basic: a pergola of the simplest kind stretching out from the house, two wooden benches and screens of wooden paling of various heights. Incorporated into the design, and well camouflaged, is the brick path leading to a side entrance. The treatment of the latter is relevant to many gardens because few things are more depressing than a vista to such a service exit. (Unless it can be made an attractive feature in its own right, it is best concealed behind a hedge or wall or planting of evergreens.)

Within, this vertical wooden framework, the plants flow naturally on one from the other, without a hint of flower-bed gardening. The area treated in this way is in fact quite small, but the illusion – that it continues beyond – is sustained by the planting outside the paling enclosure, in particular the trees whose branches and leaves over-hang the central space. These include an *Acer palmatum*, a willow (*Salix* × *chrysocoma*) and a *Gleditsia triacanthos* 'Sunburst'. The willow has pendulous branches and marvellous yellow-green shoots in spring, the *Acer palmatum* turns brilliant hues of red and gold in the autumn, and *Gleditsia* is one of the loveliest of small trees with a mop of feathery pale yellow-green leaves.

The small enclosed dell focuses on a pond with water lilies (*Nymphaea* hybrids), surrounded with moisture-

LEFT The simple pergola with two wooden benches, and to the right the brick path to the side entrance. One seat is positioned to enable the viewer to contemplate the pond and its wildlife.

BELOW Nearly every plant in this garden is herbaceous. The owner accepts winter sparseness in return for summer perfection.

loving plants: water iris (*I. sibirica*), sweet woodruff (*Galium odoratum*), several varieties of ferns (*Polystichum falcatum*, *P. setiferum*, *Onoclea sensibilis*) and bamboos (*Arundinaria*). The surrounding paling is covered with clematis and honeysuckle, giving additional colour and scent. The garden dies in the autumn and is reborn in the spring; the 'death' is almost total and no apology is made for it.

Again true to nature, the garden is basically green with flowers only as occasional incidental flecks of colour. Maintenance is undoubtedly intense – cultivating a soil which must be kept both rich and damp – but the area is small, and the end result is delightful.

Close-up of the pond with
goldfish and lilies – its
'natural' appearance achieved
by masking the edges with
cascades of ferns.

KEY TO PLAN

1. *Cercidiphyllum japonicum*
2. *Camellia × williamsii*
3. *Iberis saxatilis*
4. *Genista lydia*
5. *Nandina domestica*
6. *Pachysandra terminalis*
7. *Arundinaria murielae*
8. *Fuchsia* hybrid
9. *Ruscus aculeatus*
10. *Pulmonaria officinalis*
11. *Lamium galeobdolon*
12. *Polygonatum × hybridum*
13. *Polystichum setiferum*
14. *Crocosmia × crocosmiiflora*
15. *Onoclea sensibilis*
16. *Salix gracilistyla*
17. *Acer palmatum*
18. *Iris sibirica*
19. *Prunella × webbiana*
20. *Nymphaea* hybrid
21. *Pulmonaria rubra*
22. *Galium odoratum*
23. *Arundinaria variegata*
24. *Helleborus corsicus*
25. *Polystichum falcatum*
26. *Clematis* hybrid
27. *Cytisus scoparius*
28. *Berberis hookeri*
29. *Hebe rakaiensis*
30. *Salix lanata*
31. *Bergenia cordifolia*
32. *Sorbus aucuparia*
33. *Actinidia kolomikta*

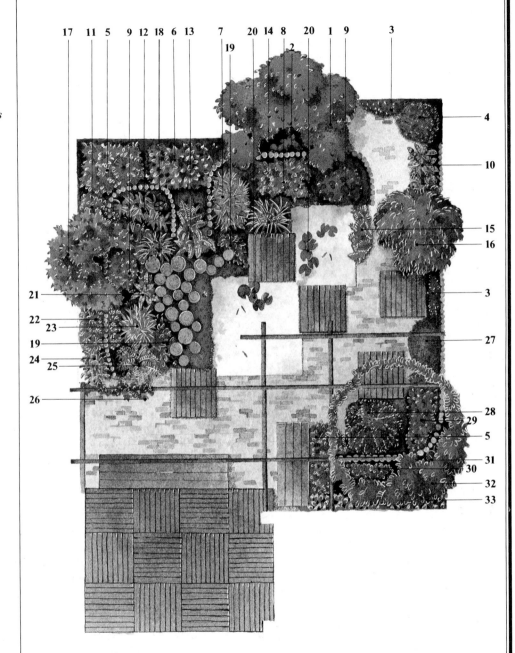

95

The
POTAGER

*

One of the most exciting revivals in recent years has been that of the *potager*, or ornamental kitchen garden. In the sixteenth century, kitchen gardens were laid out in decorative beds, rather like knot gardens and parterres, with fruit bushes and trees planted in circles, squares and other geometric shapes to delight the eye. This tradition died at the close of the seventeenth century, when edible plants were largely confined to walled gardens. Gradually people ceased to be aware of their aesthetic potential.

Books on fruit and vegetable cultivation offer practical advice in great detail, but they never seem to see that the kitchen garden would benefit from the art of design. The approach is always a mundane one with rows of vegetables all in straight lines, with no intermingling and certainly no consideration of colour, shape or form. And the possibilities are enormous, when you begin to think of the patterns which could be formed by red cabbage and ruby chard or spiky onion leaves and feathery carrot tops. Globe artichokes, for example, with their beautiful silvery-grey foliage are so striking that they can be introduced into any herbaceous border in their own right.

This *potager* is a perfect example of how the art of design can be applied to a kitchen garden. It was inspired by the old gardening books of Tudor and Stuart England, which were illustrated with woodcuts of various geometric knot gardens. There is no doubt that this is a demanding form of gardening, in terms of cultivation and care, and in terms of replanting. (Most vegetables are annuals, and need replacement annually.) Visually, it is a spring-to-autumn garden, with only the skeletal framework of fruit bushes and trees, and perhaps a few evergreen herbs, to keep one company in the winter. On the other hand, there is the enormous bonus of being able to harvest the crops, entirely chemical free, if the organic approach is followed.

All vegetables and fruit require shelter, so the first need is to enclose the area within a wall, fence or hedge. Walls and fences do not compete with plants for soil moisture and nutrients and take up relatively little space, they provide a support system for fan-trained and espaliered fruit trees and bushes, and they are instantly effective. Hedges – yew, holly, hornbeam or a mixed hedge – are pretty, but usually take some years to reach full height, and do require a certain amount of maintenance. And they are bound to rob the soil of some food and water; a traditional solution was to sink corrugated iron sheets deep into the ground to keep the roots within a confined space. In this garden, the existing old grey stone wall is a wonderful backdrop. Given the option, a sunny site is best for a *potager*, and open fencing on the south and west sides (the opposite in the Southern Hemisphere, of course) is sensible, because minimal shade is created.

In addition, the decorative pattern of a *potager* can be emphasized by the use of edging plants. Some beds, at least, should be outlined in dwarf box (*Buxus sempervirens* 'Fruticosa'). Herbs, too, can make an attractive edging. For a more substantial containing hedge try clipped rosemary, santolina or lavender as here. Thyme, chives or even parsley will give a more delicate effect.

Four goblet-trained apple trees form the central feature of this ornamental vegetable garden, laid out like a parterre. Beyond the circle of chives, each of the four quarters contains a different vegetable. A border of bronze lettuces completes the design.

KEY TO PLAN

1. Golden hop, *Humulus lupulus* 'Aureus'
2. Curly kale
3. Runner bean
4. Cabbage
5. Red cabbage
6. Salad bowl lettuce
7. Potato
8. Leek
9. Apple (trained as goblet)
10. Alpine strawberry
11. Celery
12. Calabrese
13. Carrot
14. Box pyramids, *Buxus sempervirens*
15. Radish
16. Mangetout peas
17. Cos lettuce
18. Spinach
19. Cauliflower
20. *Rosa* 'Little White Pet' (standard)
21. Lavender, *Lavandula spica*
22. Parsley
23. SEED BED
24. Beetroot
25. Brussels sprouts
26. Broad bean
27. Jerusalem artichoke
28. Sprouting broccoli
29. Lettuce
30. Pea
31. Globe artichoke
32. Dwarf French bean
33. Kohlrabi
34. Victoria plum
35. Fennel
36. Climbing French bean
37. Cherry
38. Currants

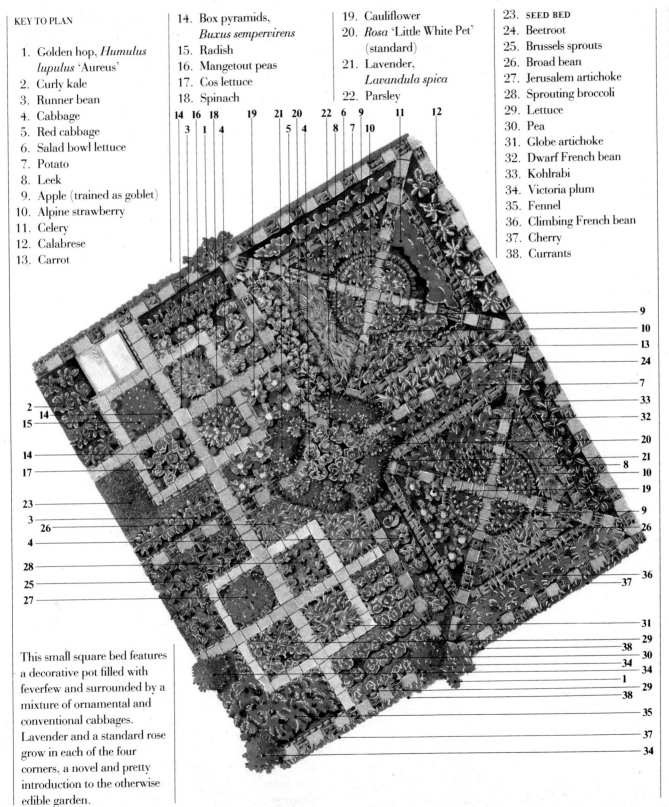

This small square bed features a decorative pot filled with feverfew and surrounded by a mixture of ornamental and conventional cabbages. Lavender and a standard rose grow in each of the four corners, a novel and pretty introduction to the otherwise edible garden.

Above A simple arbour, constructed of wooden supports and commercial trellis, is encompassed by golden hop (*Humulus lupulus* 'Aureus'). The arbour provides the perfect vantage point from which to contemplate the fruits and vegetables of the *potager*.

Right Peas trained up canes set out in the form of a St. Andrew's cross, with the spandrels filled with lettuces. Cross-bracing the canes increases their stability in the face of summer storms.

The interconnecting system of paths should be based on simple geometric shapes. When placing them, keep in mind distant vistas, existing focal points, and the siting of possible new ones. The paths should be wide and sturdy enough to take a wheelbarrow and the beds should be narrow enough to be easily reached for weeding, harvesting, and so on. Avoid grass paths which need intensive maintenance. Gravel paths are problematic too, needing hand weeding, because weedkiller should not be used near edible plants.

A kitchen garden is no place for elaborate statuary or urns, although, at a pinch, I think a sundial could be introduced at an intersection. Instead, it is a place for simplicity, with a bay tree clipped into a pyramidal shape or an honest terracotta pot catching the eye perhaps. Here, a two-handled pot is filled with golden-leaved feverfew (*Chrysanthemum parthenium* 'Golden Ball'). Old-fashioned seakale or rhubarb forcing pots would be equally appropriate.

Larger scale focal points are lovely, if there is room. One of the most attractive features of this garden is the arbour of unpainted wooden trellis, covered in summer with the perennial golden hop (*Humulus lupulus* 'Aureus'). Such a feature introduces much needed height, as do the four symmetrically arranged apple trees. Each is trained from four low-growing branches, which are tied to a goblet-shaped framework. There is no need to attempt anything as complex as this, and small well-pruned trees would suffice. Apples and pears accept radical pruning and training better than other fruit trees. Whatever sort you choose, it is essential to consult an experienced nurseryman, who will advise about pollination and dwarfing stocks, as well as the varieties for your specific soil and exposure. Growing runner beans up bean-pole pyramids is attractive in due course, though the poles are admittedly bare-looking to start with. Other possible, medium-scale focal points include standard gooseberry bushes, and even standard rose bushes, such as the floribunda types used here.

The pretty tapestry of vegetables at ground level will change from year to year, partly as a result of the need for crop rotation – a subject covered thoroughly in traditional vegetable gardening books – and partly as a result of your aesthetic sense of adventure. In fact, some areas should change during the course of a single growing season, as early summer crops are harvested and replaced with quick-growing late summer crops.

The *potager* is perhaps one of the most intriguing and challenging of historical garden forms, demanding ongoing hard work and a good eye for design.

The
LAWN
GARDEN

*

This is the only garden in the book which is designed by an architect who is a disciple of the two great exponents of international modernism, Mies van de Rohe and Aalvar Aalto. An approach grounded in the belief that a house is a machine for living in will not be sympathetic to any treatment of the garden as decoration, artifice or fantasy. Rather, such an approach regards the garden as outdoor living space, an area in which nature provides a punctuation mark bridging architecture.

The designer's approach has been profoundly influenced by the gardens of the Far East, but instead of directly imitating their formulae he has instead adapted them to the Western tradition. One can understand the logic, for the relationship of a modern house to its garden is close to that experienced in a Japanese house in which screen walls slide back to give direct contact with the garden enclosure, and allow the contemplation of natural things. In terms of international modernism, those screen walls are replaced by windows to the ground. The garden is there to give to its owners seclusion, all the more needed when walls of glass invite peering into the house itself. The designer is adamant that a garden is a cycle of greens throughout the year: spring, for example, with its new leaves on trees and shrubs gives way to summer, when the green most needed is the cool one of grass as viewed from the shade. In this garden, more so than others, the actual choice of plants – as long as they are tough and undemanding – is of little importance.

There is no pretence of plantsmanship, yet the garden is successful in its own terms: an outdoor room in which to relax.

Whatever the theories behind this garden, from a purely practical point of view it offers an ideal formula for a family living in a contemporary house. This is one of those rare gardens which could withstand the onslaughts of those enemies to all forms of horticulture – children. Its elements are of the simplest: a large expanse of roughly cut grass in which daisies are allowed to grow and flower freely, surrounded by trees and shrubs, with simple wooden fencing and a hedge for screening. The treatment near the house ensures a sensitive transition from outdoors to interior. An interconnecting short flight of steps leads down to a brick terrace with a raised bed to one side and screening to the other to conceal an exit. No flower beds exist to interrupt the garden proper, which is solely a green open space.

I can think of few gardens more easily taken on by those who would rather not have one at all: the grass is rough cut (modern mowers make light work of mowing) and only an occasional pruning of the shrubs and an annual clipping of the hedge are necessary. In short, it might be categorized as a highly successful 'anti-garden' garden design.

ABOVE View towards the garden's utility area. Woven concrete walls screen dustbins and storage areas from sight.

The elements that make up
this garden are of the
simplest: a large tree, an
expanse of lawn and
evergreen shrubbery and
hedging.

A narrow flight of back steps flanked by a planting of ferns (*Athyrium filix-femina*) with a purple-leaved filbert (*Corylus maxima* 'Purpurea') beyond.

KEY TO PLAN

1. *Mahonia japonica*
2. *Viburnum tinus*
3. *Hebe rakaiensis*
4. *Elaeagnus pungens*
5. *Gaultheria shallon*
6. *Ruscus aculeatus*
7. *Carpinus betulus*
   (hedge)
8. *Myrtus communis*
9. *Lonicera pileata*
10. *Polypodium vulgare*
11. *Phormium tenax*
12. *Macleaya cordata*
13. *Hebe pinguifolia*
14. *Berberis thunbergii*
15. *Viburnum davidii*
16. *Cotoneaster lacteus*
17. *Hemerocallis* cvs.
18. *Ligularia dentata*
19. *Picea abies*
20. *Populus* × *berolinensis*
21. *Viburnum plicatum*
22. *Pyracantha coccinea*
23. *Hebe speciosa*
24. Annuals
25. *Iris sibirica*
26. *Hosta undulata*
27. *Kalmia latifolia*
28. *Iberis sempervirens*
29. *Lonicera japonica*
30. *Taxus baccata*
31. *Polystichum setiferum*
32. *Cotoneaster salicifolius floccosus*
33. *Polystichum falcatum*
34. *Euonymus japonicus*
35. *Prunus laurocerasus*
    (hedge)

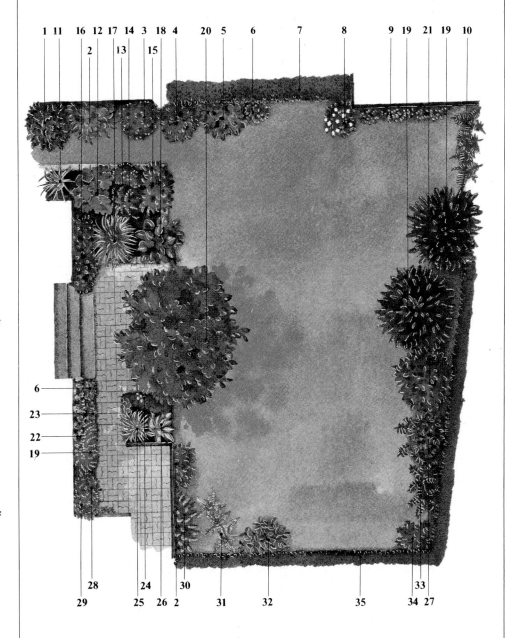

The
TINY COTTAGE GARDEN

*

For those daunted by the large cottage garden on pp74–77, salvation is at hand. This delectable, pocket-handkerchief garden distils the essence of such planting down to lilliputian scale and, with it, the hundreds of necessary tasks. But the effect of pretty profusion is the same.

The plan is simply a patch of granite chippings with a planted border on all sides. In two opposite corners are large clumps of *Senecio* 'Sunshine', an evergreen hybrid with untidy yellow daisy-like flowers, that are not particularly beautiful. I would cut them off and enjoy the silvery-green foliage on its own.

Close to the door there is an upright rosemary, 'Miss Jessup's Upright', among the cinquefoil (*Potentilla*) and lacy-leaved rue (*Ruta graveolens* 'Jackman's Blue'). Then there are banks of white and blue *Campanula persicifolia* and some winter-flowering *Helleborus foetidus*. A sweet-smelling summer-flowering jasmine (*Jasminum officinale*) clothes the grey stone walls. Rather than bush roses, I would have planted climbers and trained them over the porch. Traces of biennial wallflower (*Cheiranthus cheiri*) and polyanthus (*Primula* × *polyantha*) show that the owner is prepared to deal with a few short-lived plants in return for spring colour.

Catmint (*Nepeta* × *faassenii*) grown in a pot is a delightful idea. A cottage garden on this minute scale could be enlivened from spring to late autumn by a succession of such pots filled with everything from hyacinths to geraniums and chrysanthemums.

What makes this garden so successful is the use of granite chippings. The effect would not be the same if grass had been used. However, brick laid in a simple pattern, or stone, could be equally effective. On such a small scale the materials must be able to survive close examination, so natural materials should be used.

Replacing the *Senecio* with a dwarf apple tree would give blossom, fruit and the element of height that is missing from the garden. A little cottage topiary would do, with a few daffodils, crocus and *Iris reticulata* to embroider winter and spring flowers around the edge of the pocket-handkerchief garden.

All the enchantment of the English cottage garden, distilled into a tiny area, for minimum maintenance and maximum effect.

KEY TO PLAN

1. *Jasminum officinale*
2. *Rosa gallica*
3. *Rosa* 'Queen Elizabeth'
4. *Rosa* 'Masquerade'
5. *Potentilla fruticosa* var.
6. *Fuchsia magellanica* var.
7. *Senecio neapolitana*
8. *Campanula persicifolia* vars.
9. *Helleborus foetidus*
10. *Nepeta* × faassenii
11. *Ruta graveolens* 'Jackman's Blue'
12. *Rosmarinus officinalis*
13. *Lavandula spica*
14. *Primula vulgaris*
15. *Cheiranthus cheiri*

The
ROOFTOP
GARDEN

*

This spectacular rooftop garden is conceived on the scale of a Hollywood epic, with a cast of hundreds. No less than 800 plant-filled containers are grouped in the shelter of the parapets and steep-sided hipped roofs of the two large studio rooms that bound the garden. These containers meander up and over the interconnecting maze of bridges and steps that join the various levels. This is rooftop gardening on a grand scale, made even more exotic by the acquisition of the redundant fibreglass minarets from the Royal Pavilion, Brighton. But it is teeming with ideas to enhance a far more restricted area and budget.

Although a roof has the potential to offer a valuable source of outdoor space, turning a roof into a roof garden requires a cautious approach. There is a huge gulf between potential and reality. Weight is a primary consideration, and no one should attempt any serious roof gardening without the advice of an architect or engineer. Tubs, boxes, pots and urns – whether in plastic, terracotta, wood, fibreglass or simulated stone – are heavy when filled with compost. They become even heavier when watered – which leads directly to the second problem, watering. This garden is equipped with a built-in irrigation system with twelve separate taps, each with its own length of hose. During the growing season, daily watering is necessary, as the wind, and heat built up and reflected from the roof tiles, dry out plants and compost alike. Waterproofing and drainage are equally important. There are special lightweight tiles, such as those used here, for roof gardens, while wooden decking is another possibility. Whatever the surface finish, it must not allow point loads to penetrate the waterproof membrane, or impede the drainage of surface water from the roof. Access to and from the roof, to take endless sacks of compost up, and endless bags of debris and leaves down, is important too. And large specimen plants and trees, too, need a way up, sometimes by crane from street level.

Although this garden benefits from the proximity of mature trees so that it seems to float in the air, it is also enormously imaginative in its use of levels and spaces. Roof gardens so often mean plonking a few containers

A rooftop panorama revealing
the enclosing white trellis
walls and the bridges linking
the various levels. Apart from
the obviously mature trees in
the landscape, every plant in
the rooftop garden is
container grown. This is the
ultimate in high-maintenance
gardening, but the ultimate
gardening thrill if successful.

down on a roof without any sense of making a setting and the results are invariably dull. Here the walkways and bridges are exploited to the full, with the whole area enclosed by a wall of trellis two metres (six feet) in height. All the wooden structures, which are simple and well designed, are painted white, a perfect foil for both foliage and bloom, and provide innumerable possibilities for the actual placing of the containers.

Green cannot be taken for granted in what is essentially an artificial garden. Here it is provided in all its variations: plain green and variegated leaves; green tinged with yellow; and overlaid with silver grey. Against these, bright reds and the whole range of pinks are used exuberantly, but not in the least vulgarly. The garden is floodlit at night, so the reds and pinks, which respond well to artificial light, are ideal colours. The white wooden bridges and trellises, and the garden furniture, respond well to night light too. They also provide a fresh, clean touch during the daytime.

Plants can live for many years in the confines of a container, provided their natural needs – feeding, watering and pruning – are meticulously met. Plants bought from garden centres have already spent some of their lives in containers; how long they remain happy depends on their maintenance. Containerized gardening is a labour-intensive and expensive form of horticulture. Unless the rooftop garden is backed up by a greenhouse or proper garden at ground level, winter protection of tender plants, and storage of those which are out of season or past their best, are problems. Here, the tender fuchsias are replaced annually, a relatively small concession to the weather, compared with the amount of flora that remains year after year. Admittedly, on the bonus side, there is no mowing, little weeding, infinite possibility of rearranging at whim, and the compost in any container can be suited to its contents (lime-loving or hating). That this is true instant gardening can be measured by the fact that everything we see on the roof was created in four years.

In such a setting, trees need to be tough, attractive and well behaved. In spite of this stringent set of criteria there are many from which to choose. There is the showy snowy mespilus (*Amelanchier laevis*) which has white, star-like flowers that spangle its branches in the spring, while its autumn foliage colour is a striking combination of reds, yellows and oranges. The purple-leaved smoke tree (*Cotinus coggygria* 'Royal Purple') is more shrubby than tree-like, in its young state, but eventually changes scale. There is *Gleditsia triacanthos* 'Sunburst', with lovely, feathery yellow leaves, the silvery-grey willow-leaf pear (*Pyrus salicifolia* 'Pendula') similar to but rather

A small, secluded sitting area flanked by hydrangeas and overhung by large trees. Note the special, lightweight roof tiles under-foot.

Opposite This rooftop garden is frequently used at night in summer. Because reds and pinks respond well to artificial lighting, these colours are used liberally, but not exclusively, and are equally pretty during the day. Here roses and sweet Williams grow from a tangle of jasmine and clematis.

Right Plant profusion of the loveliest sort. The fuchsias are replaced annually, but most other plants, including the clematis, hebe, rose, hosta and the creamy edged variegated weigela shown here, go on from one year to the next, providing their cultivation needs are met.

more tasteful than weeping willow, and a very special sycamore, *Acer pseudoplatanus* 'Brilliantissimum', with leaves which open an unbelievable shade of shrimp pink in spring, gradually turning pale bronze and, eventually, green, as the season progresses.

The choice of shrubs and herbaceous plants in this garden include rhododendrons, mock orange (*Philadelphus*), viburnums, lavender, lupins, geraniums, and various herbs. Urns and pieces of sculpture have been judiciously sited and if anything is missing I would have included a few topiary box pyramids and standard bays clipped into balls at the top to give more emphasis to the architectural framework. The presence of garden furniture indicates that this garden is not only for wandering through but also for living in.

The
PAVED
GARDEN

*

This garden was designed to require minimum maintenance, and superimposing two circles of brick, as wide as the garden itself, also helps camouflage the long, narrow proportions. A successful variant might be two octagons or two or even three ovals. Here, the brick and York stone retain warmth from the sun and accentuate the fragrance of nearby scented summer plants: lilies, tobacco plants, jasmine and honeysuckle – the latter two climbers 'borrowed' from adjoining gardens.

The large open space created is not only maintenance free but provides a place for sitting, eating and entertaining. The area is enlivened by plantings in terracotta pots, both permanent, such as neatly clipped holly, and seasonal, such as the tulips, petunias, busy Lizzies, lilies, ferns, fuchsias and hostas. Near the house, the steps up from the basement and down from the floor above provide ledges for pots as well as access to the garden. The only element which I find missing here is mystery. By having either a decorative trellis wall or a clipped hedge with an arch dividing the space into two gardens, an element of surprise would be introduced.

The garden is north-facing, hence the choice of many shade-tolerant plants and the positioning of the seats at the end opposite the house, which catches the summer sun most of the day. The area near the house, which is in shade, is planted in yellow and pale green to give an illusion of sunlight. The key feature is the golden-leaved elder (*Sambucus racemosa* 'Plumosa Aurea'), which gradually changes from yellow to green as spring turns into summer, in common with many yellow-leafed plants. There are also evergreen ferns, hostas and arums, all of which enjoy and lighten shade. The perimeter garden planting is of shrubs and climbers with sharply contrasting leaf shapes: bamboos (*Arundinaria nitida*), *Cordyline australis*, camellia, *Senecio* 'Sunshine', *Choisya ternata*, ornamental vine (*Vitis coignetiae*) jasmine and clematis. An existing privet has *Clematis* 'Perle d'Azur' climbing through it, and a late autumn/winter flowering cherry (*Prunus subhirtella* 'Autumnalis') provides out-of-season colour.

114

The view from the upper floor revealing the two identical circles inscribed on to a rectangle. These are softened by an abundant planting of shrubs and climbers, and enlivened by flowers and shrubs in pots.

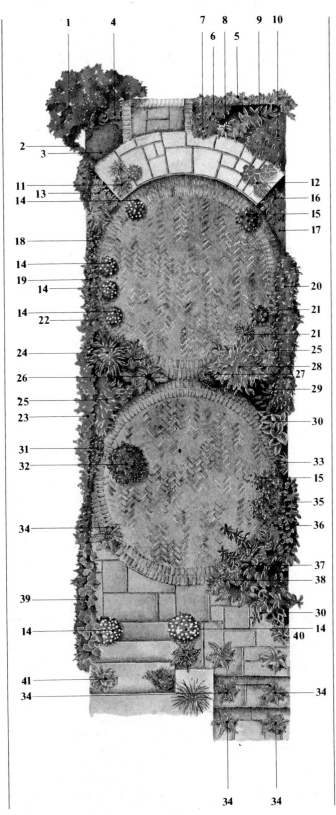

KEY TO PLAN

1. *Ligustrum lucidum*
2. *Clematis* 'Perle d'Azur'
3. *Euphorbia amygdaloides* 'Purpurea'
4. *Ajuga pyramidalis*
5. *Rosa* 'Mme Alfred Carrière'
6. *Hydrangea villosa*
7. *Fuchsia magellanica* 'Versicolor'
8. *Helleborus orientalis*
9. Bulbs (spring) / *Nicotiana alata* (summer)
10. *Choisya ternata*
11. Pots for herbs
12. Pots for scented-leaved pelargoniums
13. *Senecio* 'Sunshine' *(S. greyi)*
14. Pots for tulips (spring) / annuals (summer)
15. Pots for *Fuchsia*
16. *Camellia japonica* var.
17. *Tellima grandiflora* 'Purpurea'
18. *Rosmarinus officinalis*
19. *Trachelospermum jasminoides*
20. *Jasminum officinale*
21. Pots for lilies
22. *Mentha suaveolens* 'Variegata'

23. *Akebia quinata*
24. *Cordyline australis*
25. *Arundinaria nitida*
26. *Acanthus mollis*
27. *Osmanthus delavayi*
28. *Prunus subhirtella* 'Autumnalis'
29. *Eriobotrya japonica*
30. *Hosta fortunei* 'Albopicta'
31. *Lamium maculatum* 'Beacon Silver'
32. *Ilex aquifolium* 'Polycarpa'
33. *Arum italicum* 'Pictum'
34. Pot with ferns
35. *Hydrangea petiolaris*
36. *Euphorbia robbiae*
37. *Sambucus racemosa* 'Plumosa Aurea'
38. Ferns
39. *Vitis coignetiae*
40. *Asplenium scolopendrium*
41. *Hosta* 'Thomas Hogg'

An arrangement of terracotta pots on ascending and descending levels never fails to look attractive and with careful planting provides foliage and flower interest throughout the year. To the right the wall is clothed by a handsome ornamental vine.

The
WATER
GARDEN

*

This small garden demonstrates the enormous potential of literally starting from scratch, and how essential it is, if building a house, to plan it and the garden as an interlinked total concept.

In this case, the architect's solution has been to impose the geometry of his own architecture on to the landscape. An existing orchard provided him with a delightful perspective of apple, pear and plum trees receding into the distance. The architect has literally 'walled' himself in, with a high wooden fence. Paved with brick, the garden space is largely taken up by two rectangular ponds. It is very difficult to consider the house separately from the garden, for the garden side of the house consists of sliding screens of glass. The paved floor within leads naturally on to the marble slabs and areas of brick without, the relationship further emphasized by the continuation of a single level. There are no boundaries between the house and garden, no steps down or special point of entry; one flows into the other. Placing plant containers as though there were no difference between interior and exterior is part of the same attitude.

The area occupied by the larger pond, which contains fish, extends virtually across the width of the garden, and is edged in a 'beach' of pebbles. The small rectangular pond is a hot pool fed from a water source contained in an adjacent stone grotto. The whole composition is articulated by very precise modules; the architecture does not invade nature so much as appear as a different expression of the same principles.

The planting, apart from the indigenous fruit trees, is simple: great clumps of bamboo, pond reeds, irises and lilies. Transient flowers in pots add a seasonal note, as the contents of the containers change through the year. Creeping thyme softens the brick paving, and provides fragrance when walked on.

In construction terms, such a garden would be a major undertaking, everything in it having to be excavated and built, but once achieved, however, it is not at all labour intensive. What is exhilarating is its total absence of nostalgia – it is a garden totally of its own time.

View from the study out
through the greenhouse to the
garden. The former houses
tender plants such as
agapanthus which in summer
are placed outside. High
wooden fencing ensures total
privacy.

View from the garden at night
towards the house across the
smaller pond, with its jutting
marble jetty and backdrop of
sliding glass doors.

KEY TO PLAN

1. *Pieris forrestii*
2. *Cornus florida*
3. *Camellia japonica*
4. *Ligustrum ovalifolium* (clipped)
5. *Diospyros virginiana*
6. *Sasa veitchii*
7. *Scirpus tabernaemontani* 'Zebrinus'
8. *Rhododendron* hybrid (azalea)
9. *Dryopteris filix-mas*
10. *Buxus sempervirens*
11. *Malus sylvestris*
12. *Iris laevigata*
13. *Typha angustifolia*
14. *Nymphaea* hybrids
15. *Prunus domestica*
16. *Iris bulleyana*
17. *Typha latifolia*
18. *Abies nobilis*
19. *Iris sibirica*
20. *Juniperus horizontalis*
21. *Pyrus communis*

The house as seen across the large fishpond. The paved area immediately outside the house is used as a terrace and enlivened by pots of pelargoniums and fuchsias.

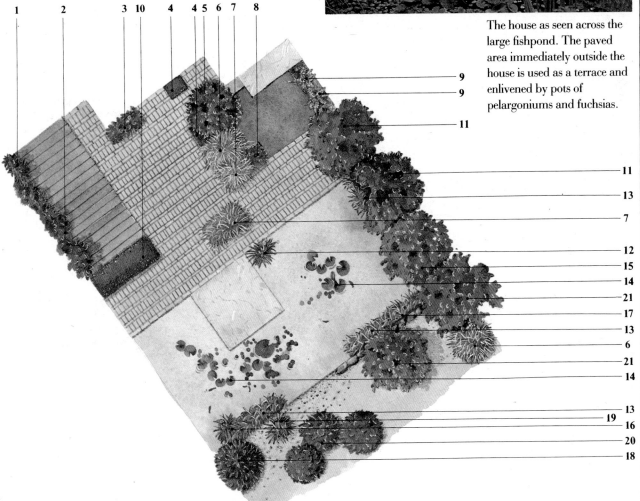

The
COLLECTOR'S
GARDEN

*

Here is a garden of quite outstanding originality and style which marries a simple and sound structural design to the demands of a collector. One pink rose seems to have wandered in uninvited, and been left to flourish, but otherwise what we see is a collection of bamboos and ornamental grasses. The result is a garden of extraordinary sophistication and subtlety whose satisfaction springs from the refinements in leaf formation and colouring of plants which, to all intents and purposes, look pretty much the same.

If it were not for the skill of the lay-out the result could easily have been a botanical garden with specimen grasses all neatly categorized and labelled in rows. Instead plants have been disposed in asymmetrical groups according to height and colour.

The key to the garden's success is the very simple structure in a contemporary, vaguely Japanese idiom into which the plants have been arranged. Although some of the plants, such as the lovely arching bamboo (*Arundinaria nitida*) grow enormously tall, nearly everything in this garden is to be appreciated by looking downwards. Water is introduced on a very small and discreet scale, into which moisture-loving specimens are planted. A little rivulet is straddled by three simple floating platform 'bridges'; on one of which there is an unpretentious concrete bowl into which water dribbles from an arching pipe. A recess in the rim of the bowl forms a tiny weir for the overflow, directing it into the main stream. Large cobblestones have been arranged on either side of the stream as if it were a mountain brook. Through them runs a series of round stepping stones in pre-cast concrete with stone chippings embedded in them – perhaps the least-pleasing feature of the garden's architecture. The lighting fixture is totally unadorned, its function and form blending rather more successfully with its surroundings.

This grass garden is an acquired taste. After the first flush of curiosity wears off, one's detailed appreciation depends inevitably on one's interest, or otherwise, in ornamental grasses. Most gardeners' knowledge of this subject is confined to pampas grass (*Cortaderia selloana*).

So easily thought of as 'pompous' grass, it is usually found in pride of place on a suburban front lawn, where it makes an awkward partner for the inevitable laburnum or double-flowering cherry. In this garden, pampas grass is at home; its form and huge plumes echoed on a smaller scale by other grasses. Gardener's gaiters, *Phalaris arundinacea picta*, is an easier grass to accommodate in 'normal' gardens, simply because of its smaller size.

To most of us, grass either means a lawn or a weed; here it is treated like the true flowering plant that it is. The long season of display starts in April, with the sprays of greeny-white flowers of *Luzula nivea*, a well-behaved relative of the highly invasive woodrush, and continues until October, with the sumptuous plumes of pampas grass. There are no less than four forms of *Miscanthus*: *M. sacchariflorus* is a tall, statuesque species with the appearance of bamboo and gracefully curving leaves; equally tall is *M. sinensis* 'Giganteus', as its name implies; more delicate altogether is *M.s.* 'Gracillimus', with its narrow leaves and lower growth, and *M.s.* 'Zebrinus', or tiger grass, develops yellow stripes across its blades by midsummer. Its fluffy flower sprays are pink, tinged with brown, and are carried towards the end of summer. Another late summer performer is *Stipa gigantea*, commonly called feather grass or needle grass. Its oat-like flower heads glisten with purple, eventually ripening to a rich yellow ochre; it is a grass much loved by flower arrangers. Over twenty species and varieties of grass make up this garden; each has its own special qualities, making it worthy of inclusion in this fascinating miniature horticultural encyclopedia.

Silver and grey gardens, alpine gardens, even heather gardens (not to my particular taste) are less esoteric choices than grass for the single-theme garden. All require a keen plant interest; indeed, specialization is a sensible course open to someone with a great deal of knowledge and a small garden. What this particular garden so successfully demonstrates is that such aspirations can be achieved in terms of pleasing design as well as esoteric horticultural pursuits.

Though a rose has been left to
flourish, ornamental grasses
form the backbone of this
garden. The hard landscaping
features are suitably
unadorned and simple.

Left Striped sedge, *Scirpus tabernaemontani* 'Zebrinus', grows with its feet in the water. Here, some of the foliage has lost its stripes, and reverted to plain green. Ideally, the green foliage should be removed, to encourage the weaker, variegated blades.

Opposite Lyme grass, *Elymus arenarius* 'Glaucus', sprouts from cobbles. Though hard to walk on, they set off the grasses to perfection.

KEY TO PLAN

1. *Miscanthus sinensis* 'Giganteus'
2. *Phalaris arundinacea picta*
3. *Miscanthus sinensis* 'Zebrinus'
4. *Miscanthus sacchariflorus*
5. *Festuca ovina glauca* 'Silberreiher'
6. *Cortaderia selloana*
7. *Uniola latifolia*
8. *Panicum virgatum*
9. *Luzula nivea*
10. *Scirpus tabernaemontani* 'Zebrinus'
11. *Scirpus lacustris*
12. *Arrhenatherum elatius* 'Variegatum'
13. *Glyceria maxima* 'Variegata'
14. *Festuca scoparia*
15. *Sinarundinaria nitida*
16. *Miscanthus sinensis* 'Gracillimus'
17. *Carex morrowii*
18. *Arundinaria pumila*
19. *Pennisetum alopecuroides*
20. *Helictotrichon sempervirens*
21. *Malus sylvestris*
22. *Stipa gigantea*
23. *Luzula sylvatica*
24. *Elymus arenarius* 'Glaucus'
25. *Spartina pectinata* 'Aureo-marginata'
26. *Koeleria glauca*

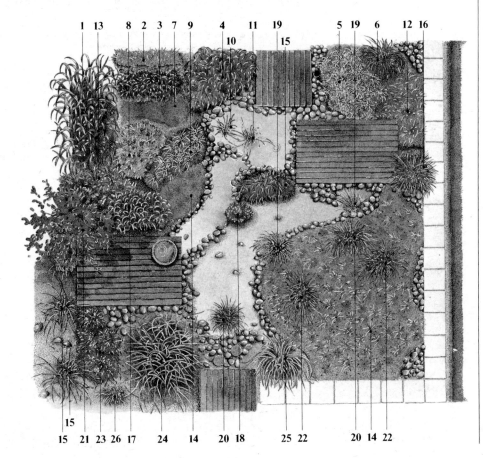

123

The
ALFRESCO
CUBE ROOM

*

For true elegance and style it would be difficult to fault this garden. It starts from one tremendous advantage; the proportions of a perfect square, only six metres by six metres (twenty feet by twenty feet). The owner's response to this geometry has been to emphasize it, creating a tiny formal garden of exquisite delicacy and detail. The fact that it has high walls on three sides has been underlined by growing a tall yew hedge on the remaining side. The house and a summer house face each other, mirror images with green doors absolutely central in each wall, flanked by windows with white shutters. The choice of colour for the woodwork is an important element in the scheme. It is easy to forget that an inappropriate house colour can have a devastating effect on a garden, however considered or subtle the planting.

As a central focal point there is an old sundial, and from it radiates the basic design, a series of concentric circles imposed upon a square. The first, and smallest, circle is a 'soft' one of spotted dead nettle (*Lamium maculatum*). Next comes a double row of brickwork fanning out from the sundial, scarcely visible under the small-scale flora. Around the brickwork is a circle of dwarf box (*Buxus sempervirens* 'Suffruticosa'), punctuated with four taller conical obelisks of ordinary box (*Buxus sempervirens*). The owner has begun clipping the tops into spherical shapes, to echo the circle of the sundial, but it will take some years for the final effect to be achieved. The outer circle is of old grey cobblestones, with raised brickwork around its outer edge, and with tongues of hard surfacing leading to the doors and the entrance to the garden.

The colour scheme is precisely controlled. Green, white, cream and yellow are used with great subtlety and imagination, for paintwork and plants alike. The small

An aerial view of the garden, seen from the house. Beyond is the façade of the summer house, glimpsed through climbing hydrangea.

The focal point of the garden
is a clematis-clad sundial.

KEY TO PLAN

1. *Kerria japonica*
2. *Philadelphus microphyllus*
3. *Polygonum tenuicaule*
4. *Clematis orientalis*
5. *Hydrangea paniculata*
6. *Polystichum aculeatum*
7. *Bergenia crassifolia*
8. *Iberis sempervirens*
9. *Ruscus aculeatus*
10. *Viburnum plicatum tomentosum*
11. *Hydrangea villosa*
12. *Hosta elata*
13. *Polygonatum multiflorum*
14. *Hosta undulata*
15. *Euphorbia wulfenii*
16. *Hydrangea sargentiana*
17. *Kirengeshoma palmata*
18. *Euphorbia robbiae*
19. *Skimmia japonica*
20. *Alchemilla mollis*
21. *Galax aphylla (G.*
22. *Hydrangea petiolaris*
23. *Buxus sempervirens*
24. *Lamium maculatum*
25. *Digitalis purpurea*
26. *Clematis* 'Madame la Coultre'
27. *Bergenia cordifolia* 'Purpurea'
28. *Sarcococca ruscifolia*
29. *Skimmia reevesiana*
30. *Sarcococca humilis*
31. *Hebe rakaiensis*
32. *Zantedeschia aethiopica*
33. *Lonicera sp.*
34. *Pieris floribunda*
35. *Schizophragma hydrangeoides*
36. *Rosa* 'Golden Wings'
37. *R.* 'Paul's Lemon Pillar'
38. *Buxus sempervirens* 'Suffruticosa'

126

deep pink flowers of dead nettle and the paler pink foxglove are allowed to break the rules. Note, too, how the foxglove succeeds in breaking the symmetry in the nicest possible way, as a self-sown seedling.

The raised beds in the spandrels are planted with deciduous and evergreen shrubs, which are largely white-flowered. The modern shrub rose, 'Golden Wings', with flowers closer to cream than to gold, is underplanted with a variety of ferns, hostas, polygonums and bergenias. The bergenias will produce chunky spikes of pink flowers in winter or early spring, replacing the dead nettle and foxglove as the rebel colour. The evergreen, slow-growing *Pieris floribunda* has white flowers like lily-of-the-valley in early spring, followed closely by the panicles of fragrant white ones of *Skimmia japonica*. Three hydrangeas are included: *H. paniculata*, *H. sargentiana* and *H. villosa*. The first has white flowers that fade to palest pink, the last two have flowers of palest lilac blue, with densely hairy stems and shoots, as though they were moss covered; all thrive in the shade and shelter provided by

this garden. *Sarcococca*, the so-called Christmas box, is also a shade lover, and its tiny white, winter flowers are deliciously scented.

No opportunity for planting has been lost in this tiny garden. An exuberant muddle of climbers grow over the trellis and the two house walls, including the fragrant, pale yellow rose, 'Paul's Lemon Pillar' (1915). Orange-peel clematis (*Clematis orientalis*) has lovely silky winter seed heads as well as bright yellow, nodding flowers in late summer and autumn. There are honeysuckles and climbing hydrangeas growing against the walls and even the sundial is used to support a white-flowered hybrid clematis (*C.* 'Mme. le Coultre').

Nothing in this garden obscures the perfect sense of proportion and the overall balance that has been achieved, both of which are visible at all times of the year. The planting and colour, of course, can be varied according to individual preference but it must never impinge on the initial harmony, the square and circle that is worthy of a Renaissance architect.

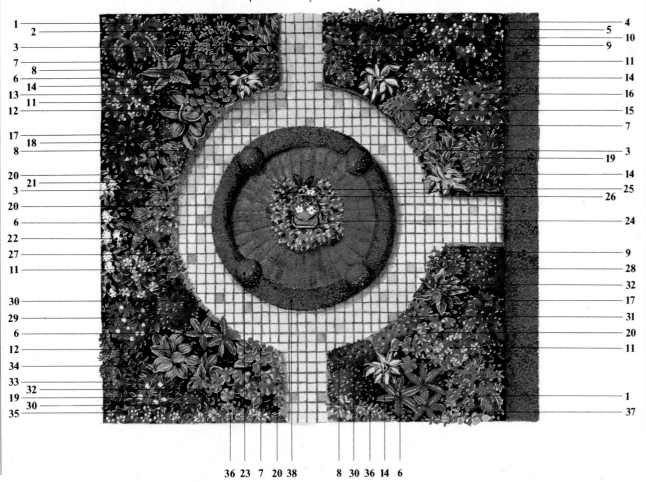

The
BOARDWALK GARDEN

*

This garden is an essay in green. It is an object lesson for those who mistakenly believe that the main purpose of gardening is colour. An appreciation of the myriad shades of green is fundamental to successful garden making. Green is both transparent and opaque, varying in each plant through the year as leaves unfold, mature, wither and eventually die. Green is a peaceful, consoling colour, restful to both mind and eye. The owner of this highly original garden fully understands this and has created a luxuriant green paradise.

The handling of the water is what makes this garden so unusual, bold and imaginative – though artificial, it has the presence and soothing quality of a natural pool lying at the bottom of a dell. It is a far cry from the usual depressing puddle, with a few ill-fated goldfish waiting to be scooped out by the nearest cat or swooping heron – a rare example of a successful plastic pool.

There are two trees. One is the rare Japanese pagoda tree (*Sophora japonica*), a relative of robinia, with similar leaves and white flowers. It does not flower when young, and even when mature, flowers only in hot, dry summers. However, its form and foliage compensate for its chancy floral performance. The second tree, snowy mespilus (*Amelanchier laevis*), is less difficult and its fragrant white flowers are a dependable feature each spring. *Skimmia* × *foremanii* is a more vigorous female form of the communal garden skimmia. The Japanese maple, *Acer palmatum* 'Dissectum', makes a mushroom-like cushion of lacy green leaves.

The garden changes character at the far end of the boardwalk, at a circular terrace, decorated with plant-filled pots. Here are plants demanding dry root conditions: echeveria, box, and the exquisitely scented angel's trumpets (*Datura*). A pergola is used to support climbers; so are the walls of the house. The climbing hydrangea (*H. petiolaris*) is quite capable of supporting itself, once established. Other climbers allowed to ramble include the Chinese wisteria (*W. sinensis*) and clematis. The latter is a modest hedgerow resident, old man's beard (*C. vitalba*), with tiny green flowers and silky seed heads – a large-

Left View along the boardwalk which bridges the pond and leads to the house. The whole garden is a composition in shades of green, with allowances for seasonal flecks and flashes of colour.

Above Clematis, ferns and knotweed provide a verdant setting for a tiny water feature near the house. A hollow bamboo pipe feeds water into an old Spanish urn, and a well-concealed electric pump recirculates the water. The gentle sound of dripping neutralizes the more mundane noises of the surrounding neighbourhood.

129

brightly coloured clematis hybrid would be completely out of place.

The herbaceous plants range from the tiny, ground-hugging baby's tears (*Helxine soleirolii*), to arching clumps of bamboo (*Arundinaria murielae*). Ferns include the lady fern (*Athyrium filix-femina*) and the soft shield fern (*Polystichum setiferum*). Other alternatives would be the hard fern (*Blechnum spicant*), the common polypody (*Polypodium vulgare*) and the ostrich-feather fern (*Matteucia struthiopteris*). Only the ostrich-feather fern needs waterside conditions; the others are happy in ordinary soil, but would add to the waterside imagery.

Many of the herbaceous perennials used here are usually seen as part of a mixed border, but are sited and grown with such skill that they, too, take on waterside connotations. The presence of water and the power of suggestion combine to reinforce the waterside role played by these plants. They are worth remembering if you do have a pool which you wish to soften. Unless the pool leaks, the soil adjacent will be as dry as that in any other bit of garden.

Baby's tears, *Helxine soleirolii*, growing on peat completely hides the black plastic rim of the small pond. Sweet woodruff, ferns and ivy complete the ground-level planting, and a Japanese maple, with its feathery leaves, overhangs the water.

KEY TO PLAN

1. *Clematis vitalba*
2. *Polygonatum japonicum*
3. *Buphthalmum speciosum*
4. *Arundinaria murielae*
5. *Hemerocallis* hybrid
6. *Helxine [Soleirolia] soleirolii*
7. *Asperula [Galium] odorata*
8. *Athyrium filix-femina*
9. *Polystichum setiferum*
10. *Yucca gloriosa*
11. *Acer palmatum 'Dissectum'*
12. *Petasites albus*
13. *Skimmia × foremanii*
14. *Echeveria* hybrids
15. *Datura sanguinea*
16. *Vitis vinifera* 'Brandt'
17. *Hydrangea petiolaris*
18. *Sophora japonica*
19. *Amelanchier laevis*
20. *Buxus sempervirens*
21. *Eucomis bicolor*
22. *Wisteria sinensis*
23. *Hedera helix*

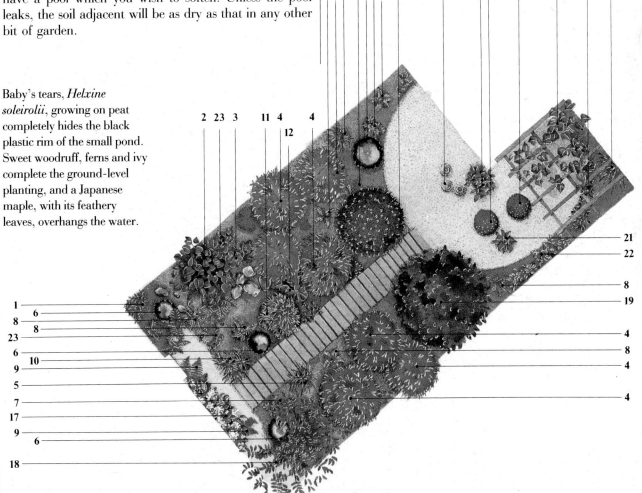

The
SUBTROPICAL
GARDEN

*

The extreme heat of the sun and strong light in subtropical regions produce quite different garden demands from the more varied climate of the colder north. Shade and water and the sight of luxuriant green vegetation, evoking a sense of coolness, must form the major ingredients of any successful garden in the sun. This subtropical garden incorporates all three elements and is inspired by the gardens of Islam.

The Islamic influence filtered up through Spain and Sicily in the late Middle Ages. The grandest examples we can see today are the elaborate gardens of the Alhambra and Alcazar palaces in Spain; in its simplest form, the Islamic garden is found all around the shores of the Mediterranean. The garden is always a court, either a courtyard around which the house is built or an entrance enclosure which acts as a forecourt. There is almost always water present in the form of a fountain, a planting of trees, evergreens and flowers, and, during the summer months, the addition of potted plants.

This garden is in a small forecourt, which has a flight of steps leading to the front door. The landing at the top of the steps gives on to a raised terrace leading to other doors, thus creating two levels. The levels are divided by a pond; water falls from a simple spout on to a shallow rectangular basin from which, in turn, it spills down into the pond. The slow trickle of water provides that vital element of movement and refreshment in the heat, and around the basin, at both levels, its architectural shape has been softened by bold planting. It is the utter simplicity of this plan which is so striking, matching exactly the totally unadorned modern house, with its pale, colour-washed surfaces and plain rectangular openings for doors and windows.

The main tree gives this little enclosure a sense of height and provides shade. The tree seems much older than the house: mature trees growing on building sites are almost always worth preserving. The tree pictured is the cork oak (*Quercus suber*); the evergreen, or holm, oak (*Quercus ilex*) is a reasonably hardy, similar-looking alternative.

The planting is assymetrical, matching the lie of the

house. Plants around the pond include the bronze-leaved New Zealand flax (*Phormium tenax* 'Purpureum'), whose spiky foliage contrasts well with the feathery green leaves of the other shrubs, a *Fatsia japonica*, the rare honey flower (*Melianthus major*), an abutilon and the umbrella plant (*Cyperus alternifolius*). These are interplanted with clumps of fuchsia, arum lilies (*Zantedeschia aethiopica*), and white and blue daisy-like marguerites (*Chrysanthemum frutescens* and *Felicia* respectively), all of which add vivid splashes of colour against the varied green.

It is not easy to achieve subtle colour effects in hot climates, where the light is unclouded and direct; very different in its effects from the softer, dappled skies of more temperate lands. Everything is either brilliantly illuminated by the sun or engulfed in shade, and the middle tones disappear. As a result, the shapes of leaves are sharply defined. This emphasis on silhouette has obviously been taken into account here where the variety of leaf shapes is so very evident.

This modest cultivated patch is about as simple as a garden can be. No lawn to mow, no hedges to cut, not even terracotta pots to move in and out. All that is required is a little tending, cutting down and pruning. You can measure this garden's success by imagining the scene without all the trees, shrubs and flowers. Without them all that is left is a pink stucco box.

A raised terrace, imaginative
use of water and bold planting
create a welcoming courtyard
and enliven the stage-like
setting of the stuccoed house.

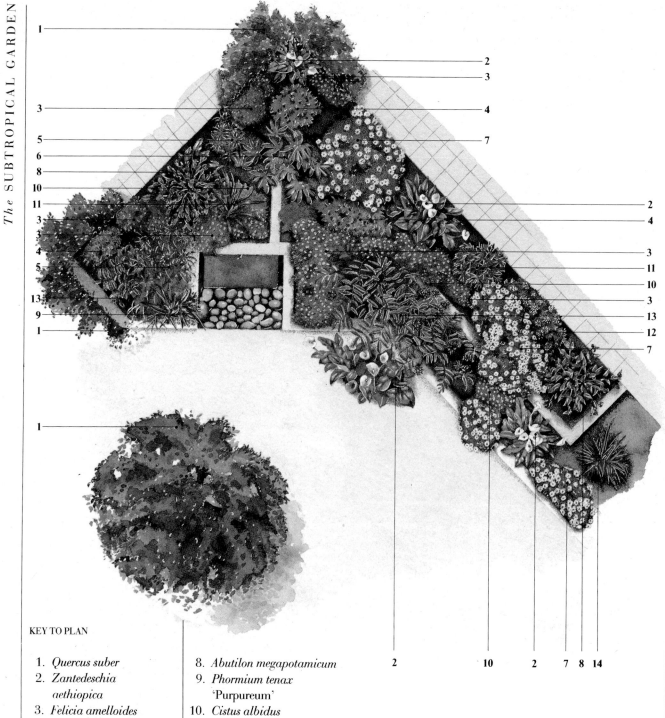

KEY TO PLAN

1. *Quercus suber*
2. *Zantedeschia aethiopica*
3. *Felicia amelloides*
4. *Fuchsia × hybrida* var.
5. *Cyperus alternifolius*
6. *Fatsia japonica*
7. *Chrysanthemum frutescens*
8. *Abutilon megapotamicum*
9. *Phormium tenax 'Purpureum'*
10. *Cistus albidus*
11. *Rosmarinus officinalis*
12. *Santolina chamaecyparissus*
13. *Melianthes major*
14. *Phormium tenax*

The large, fern-like leaves of the honey flower (*Melianthus major*) compensate for its sprawling habit and slightly sinister flowers. Elegant in all parts is the white arum lily (*Zantedeschia aethiopica*).

The
PARTERRE

*

It is true to say that most people would associate this type of garden with living in a palace or a very grand villa, but here it is successfully transposed into the confines of a narrow back garden of a town house, where it looks marvellous and not in the least out of place. This is a formal parterre of box hedges clipped into a symmetrical pattern – a garden style which reached its apogee under William and Mary at the close of the seventeenth century, and was then overshadowed by the invasion of the English landscape style.

When the western European garden tradition was created in the sixteenth century, it was based on descriptions of gardens in the letters of the Roman Pliny, who describes his villas as having box cut into geometric shapes. Out of the efforts to re-create these came first the knot garden and subsequently the parterre, giving us two centuries of garden pattern making, not only in box but also in clipped yew, phillyrea, santolina, thyme and rosemary. The patterns were closely related to those used in contemporary carpets and embroidery and, indeed, in Shakespeare's England the same man provided the patterns for both. The knot garden was small in scale and had to be re-laid every few years. As a result it required considerable maintenance in terms of planting and pruning. The parterre developed from this, and was far larger, far bolder and more monumental in design and executed entirely in evergreens. Instead of several tiny knots with different patterns the parterre is an overall scheme with one bold unifying design concept.

Today, there are plenty of opportunities to study knot and parterre gardens, either survivals or re-creations. In England there are the Tudor gardens at Hampton Court Palace and that at Hall's Croft, Stratford-on-Avon, which is also planted with all the flowers mentioned in Shakespeare's plays. In the United States the gardens of Virginia and, in particular, those at Williamsburg are full of formal parterres, many much more modest in concept than the one illustrated and perfect complements to the simple wooden houses of the eighteenth century. And any visitor to Italy will see formal parterres of this sort in almost any historic villa. What we have forgotten is that this type of garden solution was used in the past for small gardens, too, and even today can offer a highly satisfactory solution to a site.

How do you design such a garden? There are innumerable books which reproduce plans of old knot gardens and parterres which you can adapt and simplify. Remember, however, that it is not necessary only to copy from the past and there is no reason why this format could not be appropriate for a very modern house if the design were inspired, say, by a painter such as Mondrian. Begin by taking a piece of graph paper and draw your design on a grid to fill the space available.

Knot gardens and parterres require a level site, which makes them particularly appropriate for small town gardens. Town houses, too, often have living rooms on the upper floor, the ideal vantage point for enjoying the pattern. A parterre can be as elaborate or as simple as you like. It can, for instance, be no more than four quarters with a circle superimposed, or it can be as immensely complicated and delightful as the one here, which is certainly inspired by the kind of baroque scrolled pattern William and Mary would have been familiar with.

This type of garden can technically be either 'open' or 'closed': that is, the exposed ground can either be 'closed' or gravelled over, or it can be 'open', planted permanently or annually with rose bushes or flowers. (A 'closed' parterre is obviously far easier to maintain than an 'open' one.) In this garden there is one addition, a group of four standard rose trees to call attention to the central focal point, an urn.

To transpose your design into reality you must peg out

Overhanging laburnum adds a touch of colour to this formal parterre of box hedging. Though often associated with grand gardens, parterres arefor small gardens too.

the main grid of the graph paper on to the soil. Then, with sand or lime, draw the lines of your pattern. In the case of curves, you will need to make a bilboquet – a peg with a piece of string attached to it knotted at measured intervals in order to draw circumferences. In the case of laying out a 'closed' parterre everything is made easy in that you can cover the earth with sheets of perforated black plastic to suppress weeds, draw on to that, plant through it and then cover it over with gravel.

The ideal plant for parterres is exactly as we see here, box, which is very slow growing, but faster than is popularly thought. In any case the pattern is visible from the moment it is planted. It is easy to maintain, requiring only cutting in late spring, and it can be propagated easily by cuttings. Rooted cuttings – with a regular feeding of bone meal – will grow to about 30 cm (12 in) high, in five years. There is, in addition, the fact that box has a wonderful fragrant smell.

This garden has been prettily complemented by the planting outside, which includes laburnums. These have panicles of yellow flowers in spring. The scale of the trees is equally important to the overall concept, and their informality also strikes a balance against too much rigid formality. Other trees such as robinias, would be as equally suitable. This is not a labour-intensive garden yet it provides year-round interest which could be multiplied if it contained some successive seasonal plantings. And it looks spectacularly beautiful even under snow.

The parterre under snow looking like a huge sugar table decoration from the baroque age. Such a parterre provides pleasure at any season by the very precision and rhythm of its design.

View of the parterre from the upstairs of the house. An urn filled with pelargoniums forms a focal point and adds a splash of colour. It also divides the parterre, with its symmetrical scrolled pattern, into two mirror images. The pattern incorporates the letters C and S – it is often amusing to insert initials to compose a 'personal' parterre.

D. × burkwoodii, 50
Datura sanguinea, 131
day lilies, 16, 52, 76
dell garden, 92–5
Delphinium, 16, 52, 74, 76
  D. elatum 'Tiddles', 68
deutzia, 16
Dianthus, 16, 64, 79
  D. 'Mrs Sinkins', 68
Digitalis, 62
  D. purpurea, 63, 84, 126
Diospyros virginiana, 119
Dorycnium suffruticosum, 68
drawing plans, 12
Dryopteris filix-mas, 56, 63, 83, 119

E

Echeveria, 131
Elaeagnus pungens, 63, 103
Elymus arenarius 'Glaucus', 123
Epimedium, 63
Erica arborea, 73
  E. cinerea, 91
erigeron, 16
Eriobotrya japonica, 115
Escallonia, 16, 24, 86
Eucalyptus gunnii, 50, 70, 73
Eucomis bicolor, 131
Euonymus fortunei, 83
  E.f. radicans, 63
  E. japonicus, 103
  E. microphylla, 79
Euphorbia amygdaloides
  'Purpurea', 115
  E. palustris, 63
  E. polychroma, 73
  E. robbiae, 115, 126
  E. wulfenii, 126

F

Fagus sylvatica, 24
× *Fatshedera lizei*, 50
Fatsia japonica, 48, 56, 73, 80, 132, 134
Felicia amelloides, 132, 134
fences, 22, 96
Festuca ovina glauca
  'Silberreiher', 123
  F. scoparia, 123
Ficus carica, 56
Foeniculum vulgare, 61

follies, 44
forget-me-nots, 62, 76, 93
Forsythia, 14
  F. × *intermedia*, 63
Fothergilla monticola, 50
fountains, 38
foxgloves, 62, 74, 76, 84
Fremontodendron californicum, 50
front gardens, 106–7
fruit gardens, 96–101
fruit trees, 18–19, 36
fruiting shrubs, 19
Fuchsia, 50, 73, 80, 83, 95, 134
  F. magellanica, 107
    F.m. 'Versicolor', 115

G

gaillardia, 16
Galax aphylla, 126
Galium odoratum, 93, 95
Garrya elliptica, 20
Gaultheria shallon, 103
Genista aetnensis, 68
  G. lydia, 95
geranium, 16
Gleditsia triacanthos 'Sunburst', 92, 110
Glyceria maxima 'Variegata', 123
golden rod, 52
gooseberry bushes, 100
grass, 28
gravel garden, 78–9
gravel paths, 26, 67
gypsophila, 76

H

Hamamelis mollis, 20
hawthorn, 36
hebe, 16
Hebe, 63
  H. brachysiphon, 83
  H. pinguifolia, 103
  H. rakaiensis, 95, 103, 126
  H. speciosa, 103
Hedera canariensis 'Gloire de Marengo', 50
  H. colchica 'Dentata', 63
H. helix, 56, 63, 73, 83, 131
  H.h 'Goldheart', 50, 63
  H.h 'Hibernica', 50

hedges, 12, 24, 96
  cottage, 74
  cutting, 16
Helianthemum nummularium, 68
helianthus, 16
Helichrysum plicatum, 79
Helictotrichon sempervirens, 123
Helleborus, 20, 80
  H. foetidus, 54, 56, 63, 83, 106, 107
  H. lividus corsicus, 95, 68
  H. niger, 54
    H.n. 'Potter's Wheel', 54
  H. orientalis, 54, 115
    H.o. 'Heartsease', 54
Helxine soleirolii, 28, 52, 54, 131
Hemerocallis, 52, 103
herb gardens, 58–61
herbs, 58–61, 96
Hippophaë rhamnoides, 73
hollies, 19, 24, 36
hollyhocks, 76
honeysuckle, 16, 62, 93
hops, 50, 99, 100, 115
hornbeam, 24
Hosta, 50, 63, 115
  H. elata, 126
  H. fortunei 83
    H.f. 'Albopicta', 68, 115
    H.f. 'Aureomarginata', 68
  H. sieboldiana 'Elegans', 68
  H. 'Thomas Hogg', 68
  H. undulata, 83, 103, 126
Houttuynia cordata, 63
Humulus lupulus, 50
  H.l. 'Aureus', 50, 99, 100, 115
hyacinths, 80
Hydrangea arborescens
  'Grandiflora', 63
  H. macrophylla 'Blue Nile', 63
  H. paniculata, 126, 127
  H. petiolaris, 54, 115, 126, 131
  H. sargentiana, 126, 127
  H. villosa, 115, 126, 127
Hypericum, 16
  H. calycinum, 73, 83
  H. polyphyllum, 73
Hyssopus officinalis, 61

I

Iberis saxatilis, 95
I. sempervirens, 79, 83, 103, 126
Ilex, 36
  I. aquifolium, 24
    I.a. 'Polycarpa', 115
Impatiens wallerana, 50, 83
informal gardens, 62–3
inscriptions, 44
Iris, 20, 73
  I. bulleyana, 119
  I. foetidissima, 63, 83
  I. 'Jane Phillips', 68
  I. Pacific Coast hybrids, 63
  I. reticulata, 106
  I. sibirica, 93, 95, 103, 119
ivy, 28, 54

J

Japanese anemone, 54
Japanese gardens, 90–1
Japanese maples, 90
jasmine, 16, 50
Jasminum nudiflorum, 50, 63, 83
  J. officinale, 50, 63, 106, 107, 115
  J. polyanthum, 80, 83
Juniperus, 79
  J. horizontalis, 119

K

Kalmia latifolia, 103
Kerria japonica, 126
Kirengoshoma palmata, 126
kitchen gardens, 96–101
knapweed, 52
Koeleria glauca, 123
Kolkwitzia amabilis, 73

L

laburnum, 138
lady's mantle, 50, 52, 62, 76
lamb's tongue, 76
Lamium galeobdolon, 83, 95
  L. maculatum, 63, 124, 126
    L.m. 'Beacon Silver', 115
    L.m. 'Roseum', 54
larkspur, 76
laurel, 24